SINGLE-CASE EVALUATION BY SOCIAL WORKERS

TO MY WIFE SHAHIDA, SONS SHAN & JEHAN, AND
DAUGHTER SHAMIM

Single-Case Evaluation
by Social Workers

MANSOOR A.F. KAZI
Centre for Evaluation Studies
University of Huddersfield

Ashgate

Aldershot • Brookfield USA • Singapore • Sydney

Published by
Ashgate Publishing Ltd
Gower House
Croft Road
Aldershot
Hants GU11 3HR
England

Ashgate Publishing Company
Old Post Road
Brookfield
Vermont 05036
USA

British Library Cataloguing in Publication Data
Kazi, Mansoor A. F.
   Single-case evaluation by social workers. - (Evaluative
   research in social work)
   1.Social service - Research 2.Social service - Case studies
   I.Title
   361.3'072

Library of Congress Catalog Card Number: 98-73024

ISBN 1 85972 414 0

Printed in Great Britain by Antony Rowe Ltd., Chippenham, Wiltshire

Contents

List of Figures

List of Tables

Series Editors' Preface

Evaluative Research in Social Work brings together research which has explored the impact of social work services in a variety of contexts and from several perspectives. The vision of social work in this series is a broad one. It encompasses services in residential, fieldwork and community settings undertaken by workers with backgrounds in health and welfare. The volumes will therefore include studies of social work with families and children, with elderly people, people with mental and other health problems and with offenders.

This approach to social work is consistent with contemporary legislation in many countries, including Britain, in which social work has a key role in the assessment of need and in the delivery of personal social services, in health care and in criminal justice. It also continues a long tradition which perceives an integral relationship between social work, social research and social policy. Those who provide social work services are acquainted with the complexities of human need and with the achievements and shortcomings of major instruments of social policy. This knowledge was exploited by, amongst others, Booth, Rowntree and the Webbs in their studies of poverty. Politicians and sociologists have also recognised that, together with the people they try to help, social workers can provide a commentary on the human meaning of public policies and the social issues that grow from private troubles.

This knowledge and experience of the recipients and practitioners of social work is not, of course, immediately accessible to the wider community. A major purpose of research is to gather, organise and interpret this information and, in the studies in this series, to evaluate the impact of social work. Here there are many legitimate interests to consider. First and foremost are direct service users and those who care for them. These are the people who should be the main beneficiaries of social work services. Also to be considered are the personnel of other services for whom liaison and collaboration with social work is essential to their own successful functioning. The needs and views of these different groups may well conflict and it is the researcher's task to identify those tensions and describe social work's response to them.

The problems which confront social work are often extremely complex. They may need to be tackled in a variety of ways; for example, through practical assistance, advocacy, counselling and supervision. Outcomes may be similarly varied and studies of the effectiveness of social work must demonstrate the different kinds of impact it can have. These may entail changes in users' circumstances, behaviour or well being. On these changes, and on the kind of help they have received, users' perspectives must be of great significance. Also of central interest to those who provide or manage services is an understanding of their form and content and the relationship between the problems identified and the statutory responsibilities of social workers and the help given. Social work researchers must therefore take care to study what is actually delivered through social work and how, as well as its outcomes, aspirations and objectives. For good and ill social work has an impact on large and increasing number of citizens. A major aim of *Evaluative Research in Social Work* is to increase well-informed understanding of social work, based on knowledge about its real rather than imagined activities and outcomes.

The identification of effectiveness, in its various forms, can also not be the end of the story. The costs of the associated services must be studied, set in the context of their effectiveness, to allow the most efficient use of resources.

These demands present major challenges to researchers who have to use, adapt and develop a wide range of research methods and designs. Ingenuity and persistence are both required if evaluative research in social work is to be pursued in contexts often regarded as beyond the scope of such enquiry. *Evaluative Research in Social Work* intends to make widely available not only the research findings about the impact of social work but also to demonstrate and discuss possible approaches and methods in this important and developing field of enquiry.

The first volumes in this series described studies undertaken in the Social Work Research Centre at the University of Stirling. It was, however, never the intention that this series should focus exclusively on research undertaken in the Centre. In 1997 an edited collection of papers *Evaluating the Effect of Community Penalties* included work from many different universities. Later that year, a decision was taken actively to seek proposals from major centres of research for future books in this series. It had become clear from the 1996 UK Higher Education Funding Councils' assessment of research in British universities that both the quality and quantity of social work research was increasing substantially. It was also clear that a priority for many researchers - in this strategic and applied field - is, quite appropriately, to publish digests of their work in books and journals designed particularly for busy practitioners and managers. This means that the full context, content and methodology of the research never enter the public domain.

This is a loss for researchers and those with a specialist interest in the subjects under enquiry, especially so in a relatively new and complex field of research when methodological innovation and development are important. Ashgate publications provide an excellent context for books which can explore subjects in depth and also allow exploration of research design, method and technique. In 1997 as well an additional series editor was appointed - Roger Fuller - Deputy Director of The Social Work Research Centre. This appointment provided wider editorial expertise and help in dealing with the growing numbers of proposals for the series that are being received.

This particular volume is another example of research from outside the Social Work Research Centre. It is remarkable as an innovative programme of work which has tested the application of single case design in several different British social work agencies. Although, as this series testifies, the evaluation of social work has an accepted place in policy and practice, most individual practitioners in the UK have felt there is little opportunity for them systematically to review their work except when they participate in research studies organised by others. There is also little opportunity to look at evidence of progress with service users.

Single case designs offer such opportunities but, for reasons which are not entirely clear, their contribution has not been widely appreciated in Britain. For some, single case design has been exclusively associated with the use of cognitive behavioural methods, or it has been thought to require the use of measurement schedules and instruments which some workers regard as alien to practice. It has also been assumed that evaluation through single case design is only appropriate in work with people with quite precise and usually single problems. Understandable ethical objections have also been raised to those versions of single case design which require the withdrawal of help in attempts to establish the relationship between intervention and outcome.

The important contribution of Mansoor Kazi and his colleagues who worked with him on the projects described in this volume is to demonstrate the utility and practicality of practitioner evaluation through single case design of mainstream, day to day social work with families and children, with offenders and in the rehabilitation of disabled elderly people. The problems tackled by these social workers and service users are familiar: children's disruptive behaviour, truancy from school, unhappiness manifest in various symptoms such as depression, bedwetting and temper tantrums, alcoholism and struggles to achieve independence. A range of help was offered including counselling, advice and information, practical supports and supervision.

In this real world of practice the use of single case design was able to show, after some baseline measurement, what happened following various kinds of help. The use of the more elaborate single case designs which may suggest a relationship between intervention and outcome was rare, but the repeated demonstration, through the simplest design, of positive change after help is encouraging. A particularly important feature of this evaluation was the inclusion of service users who became aware, as they happened, of progress, pitfalls and setbacks.

Kazi uses these experiences to explore the objections to single case design, and in many cases shows these to be more imaginary than real. He also illustrates some of the challenges to single case design that arise in certain contexts, for example, the losses and gains which may accrue from focusing on one or two problems selected from a myriad difficulties. Single case design can also make explicit the diverse range of interventions or styles of practice which may share a name but which need greater clarification if there is to be progress in defining more or less effective forms of help.

Through their persistence, innovations and practical experience Kazi and his colleagues make a strong case for single case design to become a regularly used part of the social work repertoire because of its capacity to provide speedily available information about the progress and achievement of work plans. These studies show too that the definition and tracking of problems, help and outcomes is not the only contribution of single case design. It can also be part of the helping process by assisting those at the receiving end to clarify the problems they want to tackle and then record what happens in systematic but simple ways; in short single case design offers a basis for collaboration between service users and those who seek to help them. However, as Kazi honestly shows, this is far from the end of the story of single case design in social work. Through demonstrating its flexibility tantalising questions arise about the potential contribution of single case design. There has so far in Britain been little scholarly writing and research about it. We hope that these innovative and frankly reported studies will encourage further exploration of the potential and limitations of single case design in the evaluation of social work.

Juliet Cheetham and Roger Fuller,
University of Stirling

Acknowledgements

This text would not have been possible without the social workers, probation officers, health workers and their managers who applied single-case evaluation procedures in their practice in partnership with the author. In this respect, the participation of Joe Wilson (Kirklees Education Social Work Service), Michelle Hayles (West Yorkshire Probation Service), Kathleen Firth (Oakes Villa Rehabilitation Unit), and their teams of practitioners was invaluable. Credit also goes to Stuart Haigh and Liz Ineson at Whitcliffe Mount School, and to Sarah Adams and Fran Perry at Fartown School, for their contribution to the application and development of single-case evaluation.

The discussions with Colin Robson and Nigel Parton were very encouraging and helpful in shaping the contents of this text. The author has been very fortunate in receiving encouragement and support of colleagues both in Britain and USA who are well known for their contribution to social work evaluation, particularly Juliet Cheetham, Bruce Thyer, Miriam Potocky, Tony Tripodi, and Brian Sheldon. The collaboration with Mikko Mantysaari and Ilmari Rostila at the University of Tampere, Finland, has been invaluable in developing both the evaluation methodology and the paradigmatic perspectives. I am also grateful to British colleagues Ray Pawson and Nick Tilley, as well as American colleague Jeane Anastas, for their contribution and support with regard to the realist perspective. The influences from Society for Social Work and Research (USA), European Evaluation Society, University of Georgia (USA), Florida International University (USA), and the University of Stirling (Scotland) are also gratefully acknowledged in the development of the author's evaluation research perspectives.

This book would not have been possible without the team ethos within Social Work at Huddersfield University---the valuing of excellence in both teaching and research, the unique partnership that exists between the University and social work agencies, and the research leadership of Professor Parton which has helped to establish Huddersfield University as one of the main centres for social work research. The encouragement and support of the Dean Sue Frost has also been invaluable in making this book possible.

My thanks also to the technicians Colin Smith and Mark Simpson for setting up the computer equipment.

In particular, I am grateful to Juliet Cheetham for going over the drafts and making useful suggestions. Finally, the support and participation of Shahida Kazi in the current evaluation research and in the drafting of this book has been a crucial contributory factor.

1   Introduction

This book is concerned with the utility of single-case evaluation in social work, and the experience of applying this methodology in practice. Its main purpose is to demonstrate the viability of single-case designs as a research method in addressing particular questions of evaluation in social work practice. This is achieved mainly through examples of studies involving extensive use of this methodology in British social work. Against a background in which more is written about single-case designs than its actual use in practice, this text concentrates on the application of this methodology to practice and the approaches that have been used to successfully encourage social work practitioners to use single-case designs.

This text explores the requirements of single-case evaluation and its utility for social workers, drawing on the experience of its application in a number of evaluation research projects conducted by the author under the auspices of the Centre for Evaluation Studies at the University of Huddersfield (Kazi 1996). In social work practice, a common evaluation question is whether the services provided are having the desired impact on clients. This was the central question in all the evaluation studies analysed in this book, in a number of settings including social work with school children, social care programmes for the rehabilitation of older people, and probation work with adult offenders. A number of projects reported in this text used single-case evaluation together with other evaluation research methods, including both quantitative and qualitative approaches, to address this question.

Definitions and origins

The two key terms used in this book are assumed to have the same meaning as in Robinson, Bronson and Blythe (1988). *Single-case evaluation* refers to the use of single-case designs by practitioners to evaluate client progress or the effectiveness of a system. *Single-case design* refers to a specific research methodology designed for systematic study of a single client or system. Various terms are used to describe this methodology, e.g. idiographic research, single-organism research, nomothetic research, single-case design, single-subject design, intra-subject replication design, and single-system designs. According to

Kazdin, the term 'single-case design' draws attention to this methodology's unique capacity to experiment with individual subjects, and it is the widest used (Kazdin 1982, p.3). The term most commonly used in British social work is *single-case experimental designs* (Sheldon, 1983; Cheetham et al. 1992); however, this term is slightly inaccurate as only some of these designs can be considered to be experimental or explanatory. Therefore, the term used in this text is *single-case designs,* as in Robinson, Bronson and Blythe (1988).

Barlow & Hersen (1984) trace the origins of single-case designs to physiological studies in the 1830s. Contemporary single-case research can be traced to the work of B.F. Skinner who developed animal laboratory research to elaborate operant conditioning (Skinner 1974, Krishef 1991). However, despite its origins, single-case research has developed in its own right as a methodology that extends beyond any particular view about behaviour (Kazdin 1982). According to Thyer (1993), these designs are 'currently used by practitioners who hold a variety of theoretical orientations, but the methodology is firmly grounded in the quantitative, positivistic approach to research' (p.95). It is used in many areas of research including psychology, psychiatry, education and social work. Various texts have been published in the last two decades describing the application of single-case research, e.g. Sheldon 1982b, Tawny & Gast 1984, Kratochwill 1978, Krishef 1991, and Bloom, Fischer & Orme 1995. In British social work, Brian Sheldon was the single author responsible for introducing and advocating the use of this methodology (Sheldon 1983, 1984a, 1986, 1987).

Bloom, Fischer & Orme (1995) define single-case designs as 'a set of empirical procedures used to observe changes in an identified target (a specified problem or objective of the client) that is measured repeatedly over time' (p. 5). Data collected across time enables both the worker and the client to examine the client's response to intervention. Nelsen (1988) also states that the basic component of single-case research is repeated objective measurement of the client's target problem. The target problem must be clearly defined and objectively measurable. Case objectives are set and translated into the client's target problem. According to Nelsen (1988, p.366),

> ...the practice or research hypothesis being tested is that the use of the particular treatment intervention (independent variable) will be followed by a desired change in the client's target problem (dependent variable). The resulting study could be considered explanatory depending on how clearly such a relationship can be demonstrated.

Where possible, data is collected prior to intervention to provide a baseline indication of the problem, and then one or more interventions are implemented. Comparisons between the non-intervention and intervention phases may enable a causal connection to be made between the intervention and its effects. However, the samples used tend to be small, and extraneous influences can only be controlled with less confidence than randomised controlled group trials. Viewed in this way, single-case designs tend to be pre-experimental; at best, where repeated withdrawal designs or multiple-baselines are used across a number of independent subjects, single-case designs could be regarded as quasi-experimental, provided there are sufficient numbers of subjects to enable a reasonable degree of attributable confidence.

The search for practice evaluation methodology

The origins of this book lie in the growing demand from the 1980s onwards for social workers to demonstrate the worth and value of their practice to both the service users and the employers. The author began practising as a social worker in Rochdale's Education Welfare Service, a social work agency within an education setting, in 1981 and became the agency's manager in 1987. In an environment of cutbacks in the budgets of local authorities, and the growing role of schools in the decision-making process with the devolution of school budgets, education social workers (i.e., social workers in an education setting) were required to evaluate their practice and demonstrate their effectiveness. As the service provision consisted of direct work by individual social workers with school pupils, their families, and their schools to improve their attendance and functioning within schools, the author began to search for an evaluation system that could be readily applied to social work practice and which enabled the systematic tracking of progress made by individual service users.

A literature search in the late 1980s indicated that there was an evaluation research methodology which claimed to offer appropriate strategies for social workers seeking to evaluate their practice with service users. The introduction of single-case evaluation was described as a 'social work revolution' in America (Fischer 1981, p.199). It was argued that a research methodology that could be built into practice was now available to social workers, and that the use of this methodology in a systematic tracking of client progress would enhance practice. Several texts describing this methodology were available, almost entirely originating in North America. However, it became apparent that there were very few examples of the extensive use of this methodology from North America, and none within the United Kingdom. In the UK, Sheldon had written about this methodology, and provided a few examples of its use. However, the prevalent thinking in academic circles (as indicated from the pages of *British Journal of Social Work*) was that this methodology had some serious flaws because of its positivist origins, and therefore it could not be applied in social work.

In 1991, the author joined the academic staff within the University of Huddersfield, and found that there were other social work agencies also searching for appropriate ways of evaluating practice. Kirklees Education Social Work Service, a social work agency within an education setting in Yorkshire, was the first to work with the author to apply single-case evaluation on an extensive, agency-wide basis. This evaluation research was reported in 1993 and is described in Chapter 3. In a letter to the author and the agency's social workers, Bruce Thyer (editor of *Research on Social Work Practice*) acknowledged that this effort was one of the most extensive of its kind on either side of the Atlantic. In Britain, this became the first major study reporting on an extensive use of single-case designs (Kazi 1996a, Kazi & Wilson 1996). The Centre for Evaluation Studies was formed in the wake of this study, and more and more social workers and health workers from various settings began to use single-case evaluation. Learning from the experience of the first effort, the author used similar strategies with other agencies and found that, following some initial training and on-going consultation, and with the participation of their managers, social workers, health workers and probation officers were ready and willing to use single-case designs to evaluate their practice.

Single-case evaluation (or the use of single-case designs in evaluating practice) is firmly rooted in the empirical practice movement which began to develop in social work research mainly in the 1980s, claiming to provide practising social workers with the means to evaluate their own practice. Back in 1981, Joel Fischer referred to the development of single-case evaluation as the 'social work revolution'. He argued, 'a research technology that can be built into practice and can serve a number of functions that will enhance practice is now available to social workers. In and of itself, this development may be the highlight of---and certainly is a key to--the revolution in practice' (Fischer, 1981, p. 201). However, by the end of the decade it became clear that this 'revolution' had directly affected only a small part of social work. In Britain, for example, apart from Sheldon's work, the only report to date in *British Journal of Social Work* of a study using single-case designs is in fact American (Bentley, 1990). Sheldon's writings in the 1970s and 1980s introduced this methodology to British social work and provided some examples of its use. However, up to December 1995, there were no published studies in the British or North American professional and academic press that involved extensive use of this methodology in British social work.

In hindsight, it could be said that the earlier claims regarding this methodology were somewhat overstated, and this in part explains why this 'revolution' did not materialise. In this author's view, there are also two further reasons why single-case evaluation did not seem to take off as it was hoped in the 1980s. First, the earlier definitions tended to emphasise experimental designs which would not only track client progress, but also attempt to provide a causal link between client progress and the social work intervention used. Such designs involved a systematic introduction and withdrawal of interventions to test their effects (Sheldon 1988, Thyer 1993) and were seen by many social workers as unsuitable to the needs of their practice. Second, based on this earlier emphasis, the introduction of single-case designs in social work research came under fierce opposition as part of the epistemological debate between those who favoured the positivist approach (which included single-case designs) and those who favoured the naturalistic or qualitative approach. For example, it was argued that this type of evaluative research was incompatible with most social work practice, and that the use of measures in single-case designs was reductionist and incapable of representing the reality of most social phenomena.

This book attempts to redress this situation by reporting on a number of recent experiences which involve extensive use of single-case evaluation in this country (Kazi 1996, 1996a; Kazi & Wilson 1996). It draws on the experience of social workers (and workers in allied professions) in a number of settings and agencies in Britain to assess the utility of this methodology in practice. Chapter 3 reports on an agency-wide attempt to apply single-case evaluation procedures in Kirklees Education Social Work Service, and Chapter 4 describes a similar project with students on placement with West Yorkshire Probation Service. Chapter 5 reports on the experience of applying this methodology in combination with other methods to evaluate the effectiveness of community care projects for older people. Single-case designs are used to systematically track client progress and the aggregation of this data is combined with the data from other methods (using both quantitative and qualitative approaches) to provide some indications of the projects' effectiveness.

Shifts in requirements of methodological rigour

In the author's work with education social workers in Kirklees (Chapter 3), the earlier attempts emphasised the use of measures with proven reliability (e.g. in Corcoran & Fischer 1987), and a search for causal links to be established between the intervention and its effects. However, on the basis of the earlier experience, the strategy was changed to concentrate on the specification and measurement of target problems, whilst allowing the designs to fall into place naturally according to the needs of practice. The aim was to repeatedly track client progress, not to attribute a causal link between the programme and the progress made by the client. By this time, the definition of single-case evaluation no longer emphasised measures of proven high reliability or the need to establish a causal link. For example, the *Encyclopaedia of Social Work* (Blythe 1995, p. 2164) describes single-case design as

> a research methodology that allows a social work practitioner to track systematically his or her progress with a client or client unit. With increasingly rigorous applications of this methodology, practitioners can also gain knowledge about effective social work interventions, although this is a less common goal.

In other words, a common emphasis is on continuous assessment over time to track client progress, and not on attempting to determine a causal link between such progress and the social work intervention. The basic hypothesis addressed is that a social work programme will lead to client progress---and not necessarily that the programme would cause the changes to happen. Therefore, control of alternative explanations is not sought after. Nevertheless, systematic tracking of client progress would enable both the practitioner and the client to evaluate, on a regular basis, whether the desired objectives of the social work intervention were being achieved or not, and the extent to which they were being achieved.

With this limited purpose in mind, the only fundamental requirement of this methodology is the measurement of the client's target problem repeatedly over time, using an appropriate indicator of progress which is made as reliable as possible. The practitioner is required to select an outcome measure that best reflects changes in the client's condition, and then to apply the same measure repeatedly over a period of time. The initiation and withdrawal of social work interventions is determined in all cases by the needs of practice, and not the demands of the research programme. The resulting data will enable the systematic tracking of client progress in the period when repeated measurement takes place. The emphasis on measures of proven high reliability has also shifted, and practitioners are encouraged to develop and to use a variety of measures appropriate to the needs of their practice, provided that they attempt to minimise potential errors and thereby maximise reliability as far as possible.

The author's work to promote the use of single-case evaluation by social work practitioners in a variety of settings has been reported elsewhere (Kazi & Wilson 1996; Kazi, Mantysaari, & Rostila 1997). This apparent willingness of social work practitioners to use single-case evaluation is due to three main developments: 1) changes in the requirements of the methodology which enable an improved response to the needs of practice; 2) the emergence of a pragmatic approach of mixing methods in order to compensate for the limitations of any single method; and 3) the building of a partnership between academic researchers and social workers to evaluate practice. However, these developments led to the realisation that, in the explanation of the effectiveness of programmes, single-case evaluation could only provide a limited account, and that it was desirable to combine this methodology with other methods to describe reality in a more comprehensive and meaningful way. The exact way in which the methodology was applied, and the selection of the effectiveness questions that needed to be addressed, was dependent upon the needs of practice as well as the theoretical orientations of the inquirer.

Contemporary developments in practice evaluation

The demands on social work and other related professions to demonstrate effectiveness have continued to grow in the last two decades. The pressures from changes in the legal and societal context mean that social work is no longer taken for granted and that its worth has to be demonstrated (Parton 1994). The Children Act 1989, and the NHS and Community Care Act 1990, both included requirements for planning in response to need, and reviewing progress. The purchaser-provider split, the growth of the voluntary and private sectors alongside the public sector, and the introduction of competition for contracts have also made monitoring and evaluation more central. The resources are finite, and yet the social needs are complex and in a state of flux. Effectiveness research is one way to make social programmes accountable and to enable politicians, agencies and practitioners to make hard choices in the allocation of scarce resources.

The analysis thus far has concentrated on demonstrating the worth of social work. There is another dimension to this---the need to develop and improve the content of social work practice itself, so that it is better able to meet the needs of its clients and the wider society. The two main purposes of effectiveness research are providing evidence of the worth of social work practice, and striving to improve practice itself to respond to the changing needs and contexts. Whether emphasis is placed on one or the other of these purposes depends on the perspective of the inquirer.

In response to these pressures and developments in the philosophies of science, there has been a growth in research methods textbooks and other publications addressing the need for social work to demonstrate its effectiveness. Most of the authors have tended to be university based, but these publications also reflect a developing partnership between academics and social work practitioners. For example, Macdonald (1996) is one of a number of publications on effectiveness from Barnardos--a children's charity and a voluntary social work agency; and Everitt & Hardiker (1996) is a British Association of Social Workers' publication. Fuller & Petch (1995) directly address practitioner research, and Shaw (1996) has a number of applications from practice. These and other publications are contributing to the development of effectiveness strategies which can be applied to social work practice, by both practitioners and researchers. The concluding chapter in this book analyses the main contemporary perspectives in evaluation practice research, and the place of single-case evaluation within these perspectives.

2 Single-Case Evaluation Strategies

A number of texts describe the requirements for single-case evaluation, and emphasise various aspects according to each other's perspective. A hallmark of this methodology is that the minimum requirements are very basic indeed, and at the same time could be made as complex as one prefers. The earlier emphases tended to be on complex matters, e.g. striving to establish a causal link between an intervention and its effects, in order to prove that the intervention actually caused any improvements that could be apparent from the measurement of a target problem. Latterly, the emphasis has been on merely establishing whether progress was made or not. This chapter analyses the main requirements that are laid down in the texts, and at the same time highlights the minimum requirements that practitioners have to adhere to in order to apply this methodology in practice situations.

One of the well-known texts, Bloom and Fischer (1982), highlight two key questions addressed by single-case research: 'The first is whether or not the target problems that were the object of intervention changed. The second is whether or not there is evidence that the intervention programme affected the change' (p.235). Thyer (1993) refers to the first question as *evaluative,* and to the second as *experimental* (p.96). Only the second question can allow some conclusion to be drawn as to whether X (intervention) causes improvement in Y (the client's outcome), and therefore it is more difficult to answer than the first question. Thyer (1993) explains that these two types of questions addressed by single-case designs also form the basis for categorising the designs into two major types, i.e., evaluative and experimental.

In this context, the differentiation between *evaluation* and *experimentation* may be misleading, as in fact both types of designs can be considered to be evaluative, and neither would be considered to be experimental in its true sense. Robson (1993, p. 175) defines evaluation in terms of assessing worth or value and seeking to improve whatever is being evaluated. X (intervention) could be considered worthy if it is followed by Y (client's outcome). In this sense, both the 'evaluative' and 'experimental' designs can be considered to be evaluative. In terms of being 'experimental' or 'experimentation', Robson (1993, p.98) and other social research texts would regard all single-case designs as quasi-experimental in the sense that they do not involve random assignment of individuals to experimental and control/comparison groups.

However, in relation to the description of single-case evaluation procedures, these two terms are used here not in the sense of their usual meaning in social research, but in a somewhat idiosyncratic sense, as sanctioned by previous usage in this field (e.g. Thyer 1993). 'Evaluative' in this text refers to those procedures which enable an assessment of whether progress was made or not in the client outcome; and 'experimental' here refers to the determination of some kind of a causal relationship between the intervention and its effects in terms of client outcome. This is consistent with Nelsen's (1988) contention that the hypothesis tested by a single-case design is that the use of the particular treatment intervention (X) will be followed by a desired change in the client's target problem (Y). The experimental question raised by Thyer (1993) is not only that Y follows X, but also that a causal link can be made between X and Y. For the purposes of this text, the terms *evaluative question* and the *experimental question* are used only to differentiate between those designs where the main concern is to monitor progress and those where there is also an attempt to elucidate a causal link.

Based on repeated measurement with a degree of reliability, all single-case designs would address the evaluative question. Whether the experimental question is addressed or not, and the extent to which it is addressed, depend upon the nature of the design used---for example, whether measurement was applied before the intervention to enable a comparison of the client's situation before and after the intervention was applied. Gambrill and Barth (1980) suggest that single-case designs 'lie on a continuum ranging from designs that are exploratory in nature and offer tentative data concerning the impact of a given intervention to intensive...designs that permit the researcher to draw inferences about the causal effects of interventions' (p.15). Therefore, it is inaccurate to define single case designs as being exclusively experimental (i.e., where being 'experimental' is defined in relation to the determination of causality).

Phases in single-case designs

Apart from the degree of experimentation (i.e., determination of causality), a related means of categorising single-case designs is the more obvious use of *phases*, which can be described as 'the periods of time during which distinctive evaluation activities occur' (Bloom and Fischer 1982, p. 243). Such phases are usually referred to as

A, B, C and so on, in the relevant research literature. 'In order to discuss and describe various treatment plans and strategies, it is often useful to employ some of the nomenclature found in research literature' (Hudson 1982 p.79). A is usually the baseline phase, i.e., when the independent variable or intervention has either not yet been introduced or has been withdrawn; B, C, D and so on usually denote intervention phases.

Barlow and Hersen (1984) examine the issues regarding the lengths of these phases in single-case designs. In keeping with Kazdin (1982)'s recommendation to reduce as far as possible the variability in the data, the ideal situation would be to continue baseline measurement until stability is achieved. However, if this recommendation is taken literally and applied throughout the design, the phases would be of disparate lengths. Barlow and Hersen (1984) illustrate with an example (p.97) the advantages of maintaining equal lengths of phases across time, as it tends to minimise threats to internal validity such as maturation. The authors accept that the lengths of phases are usually determined by considerations other than that of the design itself, but suggest relative equivalence of phase lengths whenever possible. However, when illustrating an ABA design later in the book (p.156) the authors further suggest that the limitations from the use of disparate phase lengths can be offset if an immediate and substantial change can be observed with the onset of the intervention. For example, Bloom and Fischer (1982) illustrate the BAB design in a case where only one measure was taken for each of the two B phases, but with several in the withdrawal phase A. Bloom, Fischer and Orme (1995) suggest that, although equality and stability of phase lengths are desirable, where there is a conflict, the option for practice should be chosen rather than the one for evaluation research. Therefore, whilst setting out the ideal options, these authors tend to fall back on the minimum requirements necessary for practice.

Using the terminology as qualified earlier, the *evaluative* designs are the basic B and AB designs, which allow inferences to be drawn mainly on the first question. The B design has only one phase, i.e., the intervention begins and ends at the same time as the measurement of the target problem, and therefore no comparisons can be made with a baseline (i.e., measurement phase prior to the intervention's inception). In an AB design, comparisons can be made between the baseline (A phase) and the intervention (B phase). However, a definite causal relationship between the intervention and its effects cannot be established with the AB design, as alternative explanations for any observed positive effects in the B phase cannot be ruled out with any degree of confidence. Some authors state that the AB design cannot address the causal relationship at all (Thyer 1993); others suggest that, in some circumstances, an AB design may provide a weak indication of a causal relationship, such as where an immediate improvement takes place at the start of the intervention, but the indication cannot be more than in a weak sense (Kazdin 1982; Bloom, Fischer and Orme 1995). All authors agree, however, that the designs with more than two phases can rule out extraneous factors to a greater extent, and therefore they can be called 'experimental' (in the sense of indicating causal relationships, as clarified above).

Internal validity and inferring causality

Hence, a key question determining the classification of single-case designs is *internal validity*, i.e., the extent to which an 'experiment rules out alternative explanations to results' (Kazdin 1982, p.101). Threats to internal validity are 'the factors or influences other than the intervention that could explain the results' (ibid., p.101) such as maturation and influence of history. Citing Campbell and Stanley (1963) and other texts, Blythe and Tripodi (1989) list the threats to internal validity that might affect causal relationships for a single client with repeated measurements over time (p.142). The following is an adapted summary of the main threats to internal validity:

History -- Variables that occur between different measurements of the dependent variable over time. These can include any of a range of events such as loss of a job, marriage, or the onset of winter weather.

Maturation -- Variables referring to physical changes within clients over time, such as illness or fatigue.

Initial measurement effects -- Subsequent responses to a measuring device that were affected by responses to the first measurement.

Instrumentation -- The process of measurement is unstandardised and results in a change in the dependent variable, such as when administered by a male colleague on one occasion and a female colleague on another where a role-play test is used.

Statistical regression -- The tendency for more extreme scores to regress to more average scores upon repeated measurement of a dependent variable.

Multiple treatment interference -- Clients are receiving interventions from sources other than the social worker; these other interventions may account for the changes in the dependent variable.

Expectancy effects -- Clients may show changes on the basis of their expectations regarding the intervention, the social worker's skill, and other such factors.

Interactions -- Combined effects of any of the above factors.

Other Factors -- There are other unknown variables that explain the occurrence of change in dependent variables.

Blythe and Tripodi (1989, p. 143) conclude (again starting from an ideal situation and then falling back to the needs of practice):

> One can never be absolutely confident about a causal relationship to the extent that it can be shown that no other factors, such as those listed, are responsible for the outcome. In short, a causal relationship can only be inferred. Don't despair! Causal knowledge can be approximated.

The authors explain that the demonstration of a time-ordered relationship between the intervention and the dependent variable with clinical and/or statistical significant changes is a good beginning towards minimising the internal validity threats. Stable, horizontal, baseline patterns and standard measurement procedures control for initial measurement effects, instrumentation, and statistical regression. And the absence of history, maturation, multiple treatment interference and expectancy effects might be inferred from qualitative information obtained from observations and interviews in the course of working with the client (ibid., p.143).

They add that a causal relationship can also be inferred if the social worker uses the same intervention with other clients experiencing similar problems and the results continue to show the accomplishment of intervention objectives. Gingerich (1984) suggests various techniques that could be used to aggregate the findings from several single-case design investigations which are 'analogous to combining the results from subjects in a single, group study' (p.73) and 'rule out some threats to internal validity' (p.77). For example, history may be ruled out as a threat if intervention effects are observed regularly at different times.

Another way of minimising the threats to internal validity is by a close examination of the patterns in the data, i.e., the trend and variability in the data. According to Kazdin (1982), a *stable* rate of performance is 'characterised by the absence of a trend (or slope) in the data and relatively little variability in performance'; and a *trend* 'refers to the tendency for performance to decrease or increase systematically or consistently over time' (p.106). If the onset of intervention results in marked and sharp changes, it is possible to infer with greater confidence that the intervention was responsible for changes in the dependent variable. The author concludes that, as a general rule, the greater the variability in the data during baseline or other phases, the more difficult it is to draw conclusions about the effects of the intervention.

A comparison of data during different phases of the research design could be made in order to determine statistical significance, clinical significance or both. Nelsen (1988) describes how statistical significance could be used to ascertain the probability that the findings may have occurred by chance, using statistical measures such as celeration line, proportional frequency or two standard deviation band approaches. Kazdin (1984) has a more detailed account of statistical tests that may be used. However, even if the changes are statistically significant it does not necessarily follow that they are also clinically significant. According to Nelsen (1988), clinical significance is a term used to indicate how much change in the client's target problem will make a meaningful difference in the progress of the case being studied.

Bloom, Fischer and Orme (1995, pp. 311-312) provide an excellent summary of the criteria for inferring causality in single-case designs. The following is an adaptation of their list:

1. Temporal arrangement, i.e., the changes in the target problem must occur after the application of the intervention and not before. Even if there is fluctuation in the baseline pattern towards the desired direction, the onset of the intervention should lead to a change in the data pattern.

2. The copresence of the application of the intervention and the desired change of the target problem. The change does not have to be immediate, but should occur after at least a reasonable period (such as the same period as in the baseline).

3. If the target problem changes in the desired direction in the absence of the intervention, then it suggests that something other than the intervention is causing the change. Therefore, the removal of the intervention should show a decrease in the desired performance.

4. The repeated copresence of the intervention and the manifestations of the desired change. The correlation does not have to be perfect, but it should indicate a clear pattern.

5. The attempts to examine if there is any other copresent factor that could be causally related to the desired outcome. If the change occurs with no other known influence, then this provides an additional source of causal inference.

6. The consistency over time. The relationship between the intervention and change in the target problem should be maintained without any unexpected or unexplained fluctuations.

7. The plausible grounding of the causal inference in other sources of knowledge as well as consistency with practical experience.

Generally, the criteria for inferring causality is grounded on two principles. The first principle is the concomitant variation between the intervention and the desired change, and the second is the principle of unlikely successive coincidences (Jayaratne and Levy 1979, Thyer 1993). The first set of events may have occurred by chance, but with each succeeding pair of occurrences, it becomes increasingly unlikely that they were happening by coincidence.

Although the purpose of experimentation is to demonstrate the causal relationship between the independent and dependent variables, a related task is to demonstrate the extent to which findings from any particular investigation can be generalised. According to Bloom, Fischer and Orme (1995, p. 316), single-case designs have been criticised for this reason:

Although something may be true of work with one client, it is very hard to prove that it likely will be true for some other clients, problems, or settings. Therefore the issue of external validity and generalisability is a vital one for both professional and practical reasons.

Hence, apart from internal validity, another consideration is external validity. *External validity* 'refers to the extent to which an effect of an intervention, and therefore the use of the intervention itself, can be generalised' (ibid., p. 316) to other persons, settings, assessment devices, clinical problems, and so on. Therefore, *threats to external validity* are the factors that can limit the generalisation of the results of an experiment.

If the ultimate goal is to discover generalisable relationships, the evaluation report should include meaningful implications for future work and suggest whether the results seem meaningful enough for other workers to replicate the study. Bloom, Fischer and Orme (1995) describe direct replication, or the repetition of a given intervention by the same practitioner, as the 'most basic form of replication in single system design' (p. 319). Direct replication involves applying the same procedures across a number of different subjects, the investigator attempting to evaluate the intervention under exact or almost exact conditions as in the original study. Systematic replication involves repetition of the study in varying conditions, e.g. the target problems and types of subjects may be allowed to vary. If the results of both direct and systematic replication are positive, than the generality of the results from the original study have been demonstrated (Kazdin 1982). The extent to which causality can be inferred and the extent to which findings can be replicated or generalised, depend upon the type of single-case designs that are used in evaluating practice.

Range of design options available

An almost infinite number of design options are available in single-case evaluative research. The following are a selection of common ones used, as described in some of the published texts (Hersen and Barlow 1976; Kratochwill 1978; Hudson 1982; Bloom and Fischer 1982; Kazdin 1982; Sheldon 1982a, 1982b and 1983; Barlow and Hersen 1984; Tawny and Gast 1984; Nelsen 1988; Krishef 1991; Thyer 1993; Bloom, Fischer and Orme 1995). This selection is influenced by the need to identify the key principles of single-case designs, e.g. in comparing designs that require withdrawal phases with those that do not, and the extent to which each design can rule out threats to internal validity. A further consideration is the selection of designs that can be applied more readily by social workers in their practice. For descriptions of design options not included in this chapter, the reader is referred to the texts mentioned above.

The basic intervention only design B

The B design is described mainly in Hudson (1982); Krishef (1991); Thyer (1993); and Bloom, Fischer, and Orme (1995). It is a single phase design which does not involve a baseline. 'In the B design, systematic assessment of the outcome measure(s) and implementation of the intervention begin simultaneously. Repeated measures are taken while the treatment continues, and at the end of the treatment period the data are depicted in a simple graph. Visual inspection of this graph permits the social worker to make inferences as to whether or not the client's target problem has improved over the treatment period' (Thyer 1993, p.98).

Figure 2.1 illustrates a B design from a single-case evaluation project in West Yorkshire Probation Service described in more detail in Chapter 4 (see also Kazi and Hayles 1996, Hayles and Kazi 1998). The client was a male offender convicted of burglaries and sentenced to an 18-month Probation Order with a condition to attend a drugs and offending groupwork programme. The objectives agreed between the client and the supervising officer included participation in a methadone reduction programme to control and eventually eliminate opiate addiction. In this example, a self-report measure is used and it could be argued that reliability was suspect because the client would be wary of providing true information when under the threat of a court order. However, the tendency observed in the data in Figure 2.1 was also corroborated by direct observations during sessions in the drug reduction programme.

Therefore, from Figure 2.1, it can be concluded with some confidence that the client's target problem had indeed improved, i.e., there was a reduction in the use of methadone, and therefore the evaluative question is answered. In evaluation of the case, this information alone is indeed useful for both the client and the practitioner. However, as there were no baseline or follow-up measurement points before or after the intervention, it is not possible to make comparisons. It cannot be justifiably claimed that this improvement was due to the intervention, as other explanations for this outcome are possible, e.g. other psychosocial factors. Therefore, the experimental question is not addressed, i.e., no causal inferences can be drawn from the data linking the intervention programme with the observed changes.

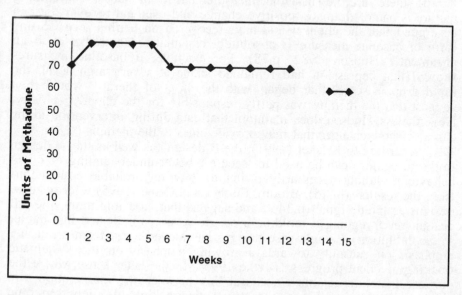

Figure 2.1   **Average use of prescribed methadone per week (a B design)**

According to Hudson (1982, p. 79), the

> simple B design is used only to monitor client change during the period of intervention. For the scientist who is seeking to study the relationship between client problems and methods of intervention, this design is worthless. However, the simple B design serves as a very powerful aid to professional practice for the clinician who wishes to monitor and assess client change.

The studies described in Chapter 3, as well as those in Mutschler (1984), found that evaluative single-case designs were more readily used by practitioners than experimental ones. However, Hudson (1982, p. 80) warns that

> therapists should not too hastily decide that most of their treatment plans follow the B design...there are many cases in which initial contacts with the client consist of, or are devoted to, diagnosis, information gathering, and clinical analysis. Such periods might be better regarded as a form of baselining so that what might first appear to be a type of B design turns out, upon close inspection, to be an A-B design.

If there are no baseline measurements, but the overwhelming picture is one of dramatic positive change and eventual recovery, it can be argued that the client would have recovered on her/his own. 'Some form of baseline measure is absolutely essential to contradict such an argument' (Hudson 1982, p.78). For example, if baseline measures showed that depression had remained stable at a very high level, the rapid drop in scores that began with the onset of therapy would then suggest that the therapy was partly responsible for the client's recovery. Nevertheless, Hudson does maintain that data during intervention alone can also show changes that may provide clues to the therapist.

According to Krishef (1991), the B design (as well as the A design in the foregoing) can be used to 'secure a better understanding of client behaviour without necessarily trying to draw any reliable conclusions from the results' (p. 15). Bloom, Fischer and Orme (1995) refer to these designs as 'predesigns' (p.346), and suggest that, at a minimum, the AB design (see foregoing) should be used. However, as indicated in Chapter 1, the definition of single-case designs has moved away from an earlier emphasis on causality towards a growing emphasis on the systematic tracking of client progress (Blythe 1995). In the latter sense, where the purpose is not to establish a causal link between the intervention and changes in client outcome, the systematic tracking of client outcome with a B design will enable conclusions to be made regarding the extent of client progress achieved.

Another version of the B design is the successive intervention design BCD... (Bloom, Fischer and Orme 1995) which enables comparisons between each of the intervention phases in terms of the evaluative question, but which is like the B design in its inability to address the experimental question. The successive intervention design is illustrated here (Figure 2.2) with a case example from Kirklees Education Social Work Service (see Chapter 3 for a description of the agency-wide use of single-case evaluation in Kirklees Metropolitan Council). A 14-year old pupil TA was referred by the year tutor for non-attendance from a high school; he was truanting from school without the mother's knowledge. TA appeared to easily mislead his mother regarding school attendance; and at the same time appeared to be easily influenced himself by friends.

The successive intervention programme consisted of the following procedures:

B: The social worker liaised with TA's parent, informing her of school procedures and her responsibilities within the education system.

C: The social worker brought together TA, school year head and form tutor to agree a work plan of regular attendance.

D: The social worker saw TA truanting, and reinforced C.

E: The social worker made several home visits to inform parent of each absence, and counselled TA.

F: The social worker escorted TA to school, mobilising parent's influence to secure improved attendance.

The measure used for attendance was the school register. Figure 2.2 illustrates a BC-CD-E-F design, which is similar to the B design, but provides feedback for both the social worker, the subject, and the subject's mother, on the progress made or not in the target problem during each phase of intervention. BC (intervention procedures B and C used at the same time) appears to lead to an immediate improvement in attendance, but only temporarily. The social worker than began the intervention procedures CD, which also led to an improvement in attendance. Again, this improvement was temporary, although in this phase the lowest point of attendance was higher than at the initiation of BC. The social worker than replaced CD with E, with another immediate improvement in attendance, which was continued during F, stabilising at 80 per cent and then 100 per cent.

This successive intervention design addresses the evaluative question--a significant improvement in attendance can be observed during the social worker's involvement. As baseline data was not obtained, the experimental question cannot be addressed.

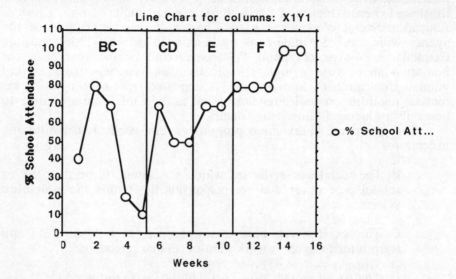

Figure 2.2   TA's school attendance (a BC-CD-E-F design)

The baseline phase A

Hersen and Barlow (1976) define *baseline* as the initial period of observation (usually designated as the A phase of the study) which 'involves the repeated measurement of the natural frequency of occurrence of the target behaviours under· study' (p.74). Baselining consists of collecting information about the magnitude or severity of the client's problem during a period prior to the onset of treatment. The data that are obtained during that period are referred to as the baseline measurements or, more simply, the baseline (Hudson 1982, p.71).

The purpose of the baseline is two-fold: a) to provide a standard by which subsequent efficacy of an experimental intervention may be evaluated; and b) to function as a predictor for the level of target behaviour that can be attained in the future. Tawny and Gast (1984) refer to the A (baseline only) design as a purely descriptive design in itself where the investigator has no plans to intervene, e.g. when it is used by ecological psychologists and sociologists to map behaviour patterns relative to ecological variables.

Hudson states that where appropriate, a baseline can be measured retrospectively, provided the measure is reliable and that the same measure can continue to be used throughout the rest of the design in the same way (for example, the school attendance register used in studies described in Chapter 3). He describes the baseline as 'nothing more than a somewhat more formal means of conducting an ordinary case assessment' (ibid., p.72).

The initial interview with a client is usually regarded as one of the single most important devices for collecting many different types of baseline information or data. The social worker usually asks a range of questions about the origin, severity, onset, and current status of the client's problem to obtain ideas and clues about how best to intervene. Virtually all of that information can be regarded as a form of baselining.

The purpose for obtaining measured forms of the baseline data is to produce a more precise assessment or description of the severity of the problem and to use that as a basis for defining and evaluating the benefit to the client from the intervention programme. The collection of data in the baseline phase could be concurrent or retrospective. Hudson (1982) suggests that, depending on the measuring instrument used, the client could be asked to put himself/herself back in the past to obtain retrospective data. Concurrent baselines, on the other hand, are those where measurements are obtained from the onset of contact with the client. Referring to criticism that to hold back an intervention to collect concurrent data is unethical, Hudson (1982) maintains that often, in the course of normal practice, contact is made two or three times with the client in any case prior to intervention.

The basic single-case design AB

The AB design is often seen as the foundation of single-case designs (Bloom, Fischer and Orme 1995) because it has the two basic phases baseline observation period A and an intervention period B. The collection of data established in phase A is continued in phase B. The extent to which the problem occurs in the period B is compared with the pre-intervention baseline period A, and the AB design can indicate any changes that may occur. However, there is a difference of opinion in the texts regarding the extent to which the experimental question is answered by this design.

Thyer (1993) categorically states that 'the experimental question cannot be responded to' with the AB design (p.103). Nelsen (1988) is less categorical, stating a causal inference can be made from the data. Kazdin (1982) refers to AB designs as 'pre-experimental', but accepts that they can 'include several features that make threats to internal validity implausible' (p.100). These features are objective assessment, the collection of continuous and stable data before or after treatment, the presence of marked effects, and the use of several subjects.

The results do not necessarily mean that the intervention led to change; even true experiments do not provide certainty that extraneous influences are completely ruled out. Hence, when (AB designs) include several features that can rule out threats to internal validity, they do not depart very much from true experiments (ibid., p.100).

Barlow and Hersen (1984) refer to AB designs as 'quasi-experimental' which result in 'rather weak conclusions. This design is subject to the influence of a host of confounding variables and is best applied as a last-resort measure when circumstances do not allow for more extensive experimentation' (p.143). Barlow, Hayes and Nelson (1984, p.190), however, go further in defence of the AB design, arguing that they can form the basis of more complicated, experimental, multiple-baseline designs when they are accumulated (described in more detail later in this chapter):

The A/B design may itself make a contribution to the clinical literature. These cases can be accumulated into series of cases which can be analysed as a clinical replication series...This is an extremely useful option and is part of the core of empirical clinical practice. In addition, if the client has another similar problem or if the problem occurs in several different situations, or if another similar client is available, then it is possible to apply the same treatment to these other problems, situations, or clients, and secure an experimental design in this way.

Kazdin (1982) elaborates the features that can allow causal inferences to be drawn from AB designs. Usually, the more immediate the therapeutic change after the onset of intervention, the stronger the case that can be made to suggest that the intervention was responsible for the change. As for how immediate, Bloom, Orme and Fischer (1995) suggest that the change does not have to happen straightaway, but it should occur within a reasonable period such as the duration of the initial baseline. An immediate change may make it more plausible that the treatment rather than other events (e.g. history and maturation) led to change. A marked change in the behaviour can also suggest that a special event, probably the intervention, could be responsible. If both the immediacy and magnitude of change are combined, then still stronger inferences can be drawn regarding the causal role of the intervention. The conclusions from an AB design may also be strengthened if the data from phase B compares with a prediction from the baseline data, or if similar conclusions can be drawn from a number of cases. The more cases that improve with the intervention, the more likely it is that extraneous events were not responsible for the change. The AB design can also be strengthened with the addition of a follow-up phase, i.e., a further period of assessment after the intervention programme has ceased (ABA design). Sheldon (1982b) adds that if the findings from research on a particular problem are that it is generally difficult to obtain positive results, and if the results from an AB design are positive, then it can be concluded that 'this is probably not a quirk in the development of the problem' (p.123).

Figure 2.3 illustrates the AB design, taken from the agency-wide study at Kirklees Education Social Work Service described in Chapter 3. BS, a 14-year old high school pupil, was referred by the head tutor of his year group because of reports from BS's peers that, although he had been absent for genuine reasons at first, since then he had unjustifiably prolonged this absence, and that he had been seen doing a milk round. The intervention was to visit the parents, to monitor attendance together with them and the school, and to work with BS to provide positive encouragement to improve attendance. The measure used was the attendance register, with the results as illustrated in Figure 2.3.

The design used is the AB design. There is stability in the baseline data at 0 per cent, then a sharp, immediate improvement at the onset of the intervention, followed by further stability at 100 per cent in the intervention phase B. It can be concluded that attendance improved dramatically and significantly in the course of the intervention. It can also be inferred that the intervention caused this improvement, although the inference is weak and alternative explanations cannot be ruled out---unless this design is replicated across clients (as it was in this case---see Chapter 3).

According to Bloom, Fischer and Orme (1995, pp. 354-55):

> There is a tendency among some practitioners and researchers to play down the AB design because it doesn't permit the functional analyses about causality that more complex designs do permit. However, we take a strong stand with this key single system design because it is basic, because it is fully within the reach of every practitioner with every client and problem, and because it provides a great deal of vital information to the practitioner.

The AB design is the most adaptable to the variety of practitioner settings. Although the conclusions regarding functional relationships are weaker in comparison with other designs, the AB can be useful in indicating change and stimulating the use of more rigorous designs that can allow stronger conclusions on the causal relationships. Bloom and Fischer (1982) in particular refer to the AB design as an all-purpose design that can be used as a beginning point (and not as an end point) for evaluating practice. Hudson (1982) has a similar viewpoint: 'These basic monitoring techniques (B, AB) are sufficient to produce rather remarkable and beneficial changes in the conduct of clinical practice. After these basic methods have been used and mastered, the therapist may wish to consider other design options that are available' (p.80).

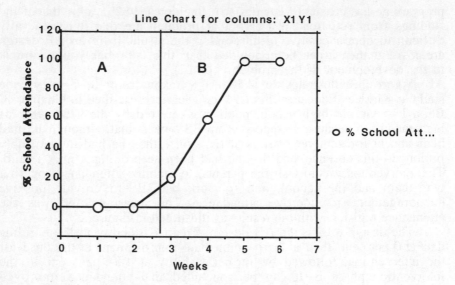

Figure 2.3   BS's school attendance (an AB design)

Sheldon (1982b) suggests that many of the problems of the basic AB design could be solved with a follow-up visit. The visit could be fixed in advance prior to the closure of the case, the client could be asked to repeat the original measurements prior to the visit, and then the data after closure could be compared with the AB phases. A cautionary note is that this method is not foolproof as the client may report untypically favourable results because of the impending final visit. Nevertheless, better causal inferences can be drawn with the addition of follow-up data.

        In another case example from the Kirklees Education Social Work Service (see Chapter 3), a 15-year old high school pupil AA was referred by the head of year because of poor attendance and much truancy (i.e., absences without parents' knowledge). The intervention involved home visits to build closer home-school links to monitor attendance and counselling AA to encourage improvements. The measure used was the attendance register, as illustrated in Figure 2.4.

        The design used is an AB design with a follow-up measure. The onset of intervention B led to an immediate, sharp improvement in attendance which was largely maintained in the B phase. The follow-up data is rather weak with one measuring point; nevertheless, the indication is that the trend in the data was in a downward direction, although the attendance remained at a higher level than in the retrospective baseline phase A. The evaluative question is clearly answered, with the significant improvements achieved in school attendance. The changes in the trend in the data (as described) suggest that the intervention probably caused the changes, although alternative explanations cannot be ruled out with any confidence because of the limitations of the follow-up data. A still greater degree of experimentation would require the ABA design, with a return to baseline following intervention. The difference between the AB+follow-up and the ABA design is that, whereas in the former the follow-up could be at one or more points during a reasonable period following the intervention, in the ABA design the measure is administered repeatedly in the same way throughout the period covered by the A, B, and the second A phases.

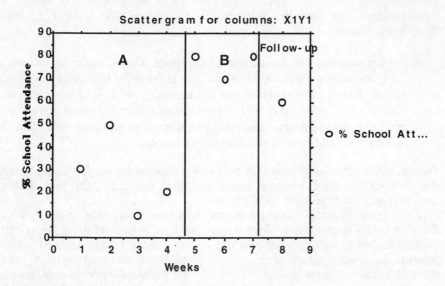

Figure 2.4   AA's school attendance (an AB+follow-up design)

The basic experimental design ABA

The ABA design is the simplest of the experimental analysis strategies in which the independent variable is introduced and then withdrawn (Barlow and Hersen, 1984). The first two phases of this design are exactly the same as the AB design, enabling comparisons of the 'before' and 'after' phases. With the ABA (or withdrawal) design, however, the practitioner decides to return to baseline conditions---the second A phase. Now it is possible to make two comparisons: 1) between the first baseline and the intervention; and 2) between the intervention and the second baseline. The hypothesis to be tested is that the intervention is the causal ingredient for change in phase B, and this can be demonstrated if the target problem changes in the direction it was before the intervention phase. Unless the natural history of the target problem were to follow similar fluctuations in trends, threats to internal validity can be minimised with greater confidence. Unlike the AB designs, the ABA designs are accepted as being experimental by all the texts, although they are considered to be so at a rather tentative level. They still do not preclude alternative explanations such as history, except at a higher level of probability than the AB designs.

The experimental nature of ABA designs, though rather basic, is explained by Hersen and Barlow (1976, p. 176). If after the baseline measurement A, the application of the treatment B leads to improvement, and then the subsequent withdrawal (the second A) leads to a deterioration,

> one can conclude with a high degree of certainty that the treatment variable is the agent responsible for observed changes in the target behaviour. Unless the natural history of the behaviour under study were to follow identical fluctuations in trends, it is most improbable that observed changes are due to any influence (e.g., some correlated or uncontrolled variable) other than the treatment variable that is systematically changed.

Hence, stronger conclusions can be drawn than with the AB design, with the proviso that the B phase is not too long in order to minimise history and maturation (Sheldon 1982b).

In another case example from Kirklees Education Social Work Service (see Chapter 3), a 13-year old pupil AW was referred by a high school for erratic attendance and the use of forged letters allegedly from parents to cover the absences. There had been no improvement even after the parents were made aware of the situation. AW's disaffection had increased further by continuous reference to the absences by teachers when he did go to school. The intervention was aimed at improving attendance through counselling and liaison with school staff to make school a more positive experience for AW. Attendance was rewarded by extra help with biology (a subject singled out by AW as the most problematic), praise from teachers, a quantity of snooker chalk after a full-week of attendance, and coffee and cakes from the social worker following significant improvements. The measure used was the attendance register and the results are illustrated as an ABA design in Figure 2.5. The onset of intervention (B) demonstrates a marked improvement; the withdrawal (second A) shows that although some effects were maintained, the trend in the data reflected a worsening situation, allowing inferences to be drawn with some confidence that the improvements in phase B were due to the intervention.

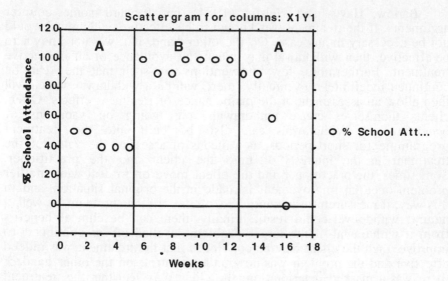

Figure 2.5   AW's school attendance (an ABA design)

Tawny and Gast (1984) describe some limitations of the ABA design. First is the susceptibility to numerous threats to internal and external validity, e.g. the possibility, although remote, that the ABA phases coincided with the naturally occurring cyclical variations of the target problem, as indicated by Hersen and Barlow (1976) above. This can be controlled by introducing a fourth phase, namely another B--the ABAB design described below. Second, the dependent variable levels observed in the first A phase may not be fully retrieved in the second A phase due to placebo effects, although they can be approximated. Third, this design cannot be used to establish causality where the dependent variable is difficult if not impossible to reverse, e.g. academic skills. Finally, there are practical and ethical problems associated with terminating a study in a baseline or withdrawal phase.

Withdrawal is described as an 'experimental' course of action by Barlow, Hayes and Nelson (1984): 'If improvement then slows or actually reverses, one can conclude that a treatment effect is likely' (p.191). However, the removal of a successful intervention may raise fundamental ethical questions and may not be desirable in many cases. For example, if the intervention is withdrawn for the purpose of experimentation, is the client expected to unlearn the effects of the intervention phase (Sheldon 1982b)? In any case, if an effective treatment is withdrawn purely for experimental purposes, then the withdrawal obviously raises ethical issues.

Barlow, Hayes and Nelson (1984) put forward some counter arguments. If the treatment was known to be effective, withdrawal would not be necessary in any case. On the other hand, if it was not known to be effective, then withdrawal may mean the avoidance of an ineffective treatment. Furthermore, few interventions are such that they can be continued indefinitely; eventually, there will be a withdrawal, which will then allow an assessment of the maintenance of treatment effects. Often, clients themselves create withdrawals, e.g. going on vacations or becoming ill. Withdrawals can also be built into the treatment programme for short periods, as a means of assessing the value of the treatment in the interests of both the client and the practitioner. Sometimes, the practitioner and the client move on to deal with another problem once an improvement is made in the original situation, and in this way, if measurement is continued of the original problem as well, a natural withdrawal could result. Finally, there can be clinical benefits from a withdrawal--if the target problem levelled off or continued to improve, then the client may be convinced that the treatment was indeed effective and the problem was now under control; on the other hand, if there was a marked deterioration, the client may feel that the treatment was effective and is still necessary. 'Thus, appropriately handled, withdrawals can be a kind of testing ground both for the clinician and for the client' (ibid., p.193). Nevertheless, if ethical and practical considerations make withdrawal phases undesirable, and the purpose of the evaluation is to establish causal relationships, than more sophisticated designs (e.g. multiple baseline strategies) can be used that do not require withdrawal phases, essentially involving replication of the AB design across more than one client or across more than one target problem.

Bloom and Fischer (1982) also emphasise that interventions do come to an end and therefore one approach may be to use the AB design and have a follow-up second A phase. The second baseline phase can then be viewed as simply termination with continued monitoring of the problem, which is more consistent with the needs of the client and the practitioner. Barlow, Hayes and Nelson (1984) point out that as far as the second A phase is concerned, it is impossible to return to baseline like in the first A in a literal sense. In fact, the second baseline phase immediately follows an AB sequence, and therefore whilst the second A must be similar functionally to the first A, it cannot be identical in form. Carry-over effects from the B phase--or the placebo effect--are likely in the second A phase, which could be viewed rather more as an extinction than a withdrawal. It is the trend in the data over the three phases, rather than the absolute levels, that allow conclusions to be drawn regarding experimentation. If the application of intervention B produces a desired change, and withdrawal of B leads to a reduction in these desired behaviours, then with two changes (the ABA design) in the data patterns rather than one (the AB design). The ABA design enables the researcher to 'establish a higher degree of confidence' (Jayaratne and Levy, 1979, p.139).

Although the ABA design is considered to be an experimental design, Barlow and Hersen (1984) suggest that the purpose of the second A is to confirm the effects of the independent variable (i.e. establish a degree of internal validity) rather than to generalise (or to replicate) the clinical situation---for the latter, a greater degree of experimentation may be necessary. For example, to counter-balance the irreversibility of learned events or the carry-over effects of the first intervention phase, the use of more sophisticated designs is recommended in the texts referred to above, e.g. the ABAB design where another B phase is introduced. Another way is through the replication of the ABA design in different subjects which further strengthens the conclusions regarding the controlling forces of the intervention, as it is unlikely that every subject would have changed in that same direction by chance alone (Bloom and Fischer, 1982). Jayaratne and Levy (1979, p. 151-2) describe such a replication of the ABA design across three subjects. Chapter 3 of this book illustrates further examples from a groupwork project at Fartown School where the ABA design was used.

A variation of the ABA design is the BAB design, as described in Thyer (1993), Barlow and Hersen (1984) and Bloom and Fischer (1982). If the baseline period A is not possible at the initial stage for ethical or other reasons of practice which do not allow the intervention to be postponed, then the BAB would be an appropriate design to use under such circumstances. The design begins with an intervention phase, then it is removed for a period, and then it ends in another intervention phase, allowing two comparisons to be made: first, of the B phase with the subsequent A; and second, between the A and the second intervention phase B.

According to Thyer (1993), 'In a sense, the BAB design has twice the potential internal validity of the AB design alone, because two data shifts (or coincidental changes) are possible, as opposed to only one in the AB design' (p.108). Bloom and Fischer (1982) recommend the BAB design almost as much as the more powerful ABAB design. Kazdin (1982) suggests that the ABAB design could begin with an intervention phase and continue as BABA, without changing the logic of the design with regard to the alternating phases. Bloom and Fischer (1982) point out that a major limitation of the BAB design is the same as that of other withdrawal designs, i.e., the suitability of withdrawing a successful intervention.

The experimental replication design ABAB

The distinctive feature of this design is that the first two phases are repeated in the second two phases, hence the label 'experimental replication' (Bloom and Fischer, 1982, p.314). The ABAB is also called a 'withdrawal design' (Thyer 1993, p.104). Essentially, this design builds on the AB and ABA designs by adding a fourth phase---the second intervention phase B. The AB phases tell the practitioner about the changes occurring   presumably as a result of the intervention applied. In the third phase (the second A), removal of intervention provides stronger evidence that the intervention was functionally linked with the changes observed in the client's target   problem. By adding a fourth phase (second B), a third source of evidence regarding the causal nature of the intervention is introduced. This protects the design from several threats to internal validity (e.g. extraneous events, events occurring within the client system, and changes brought about by the testing itself), and allows a greater degree of experimentation than in the AB and ABA designs. According to Thyer (1993, p. 104), experimental single-case designs 'attempt to control for rival hypotheses by demonstrating that there was more than one coincidence in which treatment began and then the client system improved or in which the treatment was discontinued and the client deteriorated'. One such relationship may plausibly be attributable to coincidence (as in the AB design), but if the researcher is able to demonstrate that there were 'two or more times in which improvement in a target problem began only after a given treatment was initiated, the potential relevance of rival explanations is greatly reduced'.

All the texts referred to above point out that if this design (like the AB and ABA above) is replicated across clients with the same target problems using the same intervention, the causal relationships found would be even more conclusive.

The ABAB design is illustrated in a case example, again   from Kirklees Education Social Work Service. AR, aged 14 years, was referred by the high school for persistent absenteeism. The intervention (B phases in Figure 2.6) consisted of counselling for both AR and his family,   building   better   home-school   links,   and   providing encouragement for AR in school. The measure used was the school attendance register which is recorded twice a day; AR's actual attendance is represented in Figure 2.6 as a percentage of the total possible attendance per week.

In fact, Figure 2.6 illustrates an ABABA design which is stronger than the classical ABAB experimental design because it ends with a further 'return to baseline' phase A. The first (retrospective) baseline is not stable, but indicates that attendance varied from nil to 40 per cent. At the onset of the first intervention phase B, an immediate improvement took place   which   was   largely   maintained. When   the   intervention   was withdrawn,   attendance   once   again   deteriorated,   but   improved dramatically when the intervention   was   re-introduced. The follow-up phase A at the end of the intervention indicates that although   attendance was deteriorating again, it was still higher than the initial baseline. The evaluative question is addressed because the improvements in attendance are clearly presented. The experimental question (i.e., whether the intervention was responsible for the improvements) is also addressed because of the four successive 'coincidences'. Using the 'principle of unlikely successive coincidences' (Thyer 1993, p.105), it can be concluded that the intervention was the only plausible explanation for these changes, i.e., this illustration of the ABAB design possesses a higher degree of internal validity than the AB and ABA designs. Here, it should be noted that the withdrawal phases were instituted not because of research; they occurred naturally in the course of practice due to the social worker's strategy of caseload management.

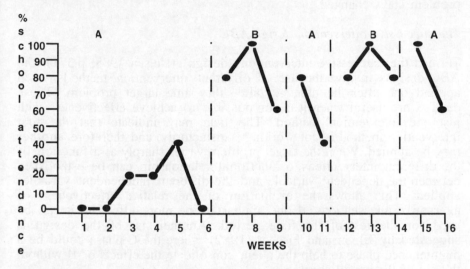

Figure 2.6   **AR's school attendance (an ABABA design)**
Source: *Kazi (1996a)*

According to Bloom and Fischer (1982), the ABAB has similar ethical problems as the ABA with the withdrawal phase, but this is offset by the fact that it ends in an intervention phase. However, this design may be too cumbersome and time-consuming, and it may not be possible in practice to maintain equal lengths of the four phases (although this is not a necessary condition as clear trends in the data at the start and end of the phases could compensate for the unequal lengths of the phases). This design also suffers from carry-over effects from the first intervention to the next---for example, if the stability and the trend in the data during the second A phase is such that it is not obvious that the trend is clearly away from the intervention phase and toward the original baseline level, then carry-over effects have probably occurred. In practice, carry-over effects (e.g. well learnt behaviour following the first intervention phase) are advantageous in that if they were strong, the experiment could end in the third phase which then becomes a follow-up and termination phase; however, it then weakens the conclusion that the intervention itself caused the changes. Carry-over effects could be reduced by shortening the length of the phases, as longer ones may allow enough time for the establishment of new conditioned reinforcers. Bloom and Fischer (1982) recommend that if the phases cannot be equal because of various practice considerations, then the second B phase should be the longest and the second A the shortest to minimise the withdrawal period and to ensure that the problem stays changed.

The successive intervention design ABC

Termed the 'successive interventions design' (Nelsen 1988, p.371), the ABC designs involve the use of different intervention methods, each applied one after the other to alter the same target problem. These designs are useful when it is not possible to achieve effectiveness with just one intervention method. The data may indicate that the first intervention method is not working satisfactorily, and therefore another may be applied. When the target problem varies sharply as a function of the different interventions, a functional relationship can be established between the dependent variable and the different independent variables applied. This allows the evaluation of the relative effectiveness of alternative interventions; if one appears to be more effective, it can be used for the rest of the time period. Another use of the design is suggested by Bloom and Fischer (1982) where the C phase could be a maintenance phase to help the client consolidate the effects of B without the aid of the practitioner.

Figure 2.7 illustrates an A-B-BC-C successive intervention design, from the Kirklees Education Social Work Service. JH, a 15-year old high school pupil, was referred by the school's year tutor for persistent absenteeism. JH's attendance had been erratic since starting at high school and she had been referred to the social worker on many previous occasions. Over the four months prior to the latest referral, her attendance deteriorated from 60 per cent to 10 per cent. In this period, JH began a relationship with a new boyfriend and after lots of arguments at home, left home and moved in with him and some other people. Her mother was unable to contact her and she did not attend school. Now she had returned home, but her mother was not sure if she could cope with JH and had requested help from the social worker. The intervention was to effect a gradual introduction back to school and to arrange positive encouragement from teachers (C). The social worker also provided weekly counselling sessions for grandmother, mother, JH and boyfriend for seven weeks (B). The measure used for school attendance was the register (Figure 2.7).

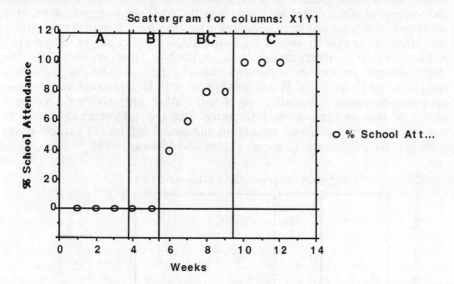

Figure 2.7   JH's school attendance (an A-B-BC-C design)

A self-anchored rating scale was also used to determine mother's feelings about the relationship with her daughter. On a five-point scale ranging from 'very bad relationship' (1) to 'very good relationship' (5), the results were as illustrated in Figure 2.8.

Figure 2.7 illustrates an A-B-BC-C design which is similar to the AB design but includes more than one intervention phase. The retrospective baseline data is stable throughout at 0 per cent. The onset of intervention procedure B did not effect an improvement, but when B was combined with intervention C, there was an immediate, sharp improvement which continued throughout the BC phase. When B was withdrawn, but C was still continuing, another dramatic improvement can be observed, the attendance now remaining stable at 100 per cent. The evaluative question is clearly answered; it can be concluded that there were dramatic, significant improvements in attendance from BC onwards. The trend in the data (stability at 0 per cent in A and 100 per cent in C) provides a strong hint that the intervention C (when preceded by B) was responsible for these improvements, although alternative explanations may be possible. However, this design was replicated (with the exception of the C phase) across the other target problem---mother's feelings about her relationship with JH (Figure 2.8), which indicates that there was an immediate improvement at the onset of B, which then tapered off; and when BC was introduced, another immediate, sharp improvement took place which then continued throughout phase BC. It can be concluded, therefore, that significant improvements were also achieved in this second dependent variable. Figure 2.8 indicates a strong hint that although B was not immediately effective in improving attendance, the intervention was probably responsible for the improvement in mother's feelings about the relationship with her daughter, and that when B was combined with C, this combination was probably responsible for effecting a still further improvement. As there are now two designs, both indicating that the intervention(s) led to improvements in two target problems, the causal inferences can be made with greater confidence (Barlow, Hayes and Nelson 1984).

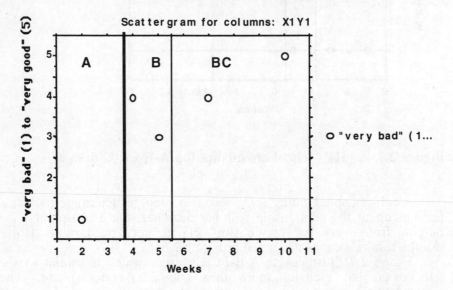

Figure 2.8   Mother's feelings about relationship with daughter (an A-B-BC design)

Nelsen (1988) considers the ABC... to be more complex than B and AB, but adds that the findings can be no more definitive than with the AB design as the possible effects of intervening variables cannot be accounted for. Nevertheless, Bloom and Fischer (1982)'s contention is that if data from the phase B indicate a stable positive change as compared to A, then observing clear changes after C provides a hint of causal factors; but they accept that the design does not offer a clear basis for making such a claim because the phases are non-adjacent.

Moreover, the changes in phase C may be due to cumulative effects from phase B. The conclusions regarding causal relationships can only be tentative and weak, as in the AB design. A variation is ABAC, where the full effects of B can be analysed by comparing it with the two baselines, but the full effects of C can only be determined with a third baseline phase in an ABACA design.

The periodic treatment elements design PTD

A variant of this design is called 'periodic treatments element' (PTD) by Barlow, Hayes and Nelsen (1984) which, like the ABC designs, requires no withdrawal phases. If the practitioner sees the client on a weekly basis, when is the treatment present? Does it continue on to the next session? The authors raise these questions and then reply that most practitioners would hold a 'continuous, rather than a digital, perspective' (p.210). The periodic treatments design draws upon this, with the

> notion that a consistent relationship between periodicity of treatment sessions and periodicity of behaviour change can demonstrate therapeutic effects. It can be used when the frequency of measurement far exceeds the frequency of treatment sessions. The PTD is particularly useful when the treatment sessions are irregularly scheduled, so that normal periodicity cannot mimic true effects. If treatment is more rapid in a given period following treatment than at other times, then a treatment effect can be identified. For example, there may be sudden improvements or jumps in the data following treatment. If this is consistent, despite irregular spacing of treatment sessions, the sessions are probably responsible (p.211).

The authors point out later that the PTD views time from treatment as a continuous treatment-related variable which is then compared to the outcome variable. Delayed effects, if consistent, can also be related to the treatment.

Figure 2.9 illustrates the PTD design with a case example from a truancy and disaffection project based at a school in Kirklees Metropolitan Council (Kazi, Craven and Wilson 1995). The education social worker's intervention programme in the case of EH is presented in the form of seven specific events, including home visits, letters, meeting with parents and EH, and counselling. Figure 2.9 indicates that progress was made in school attendance after each of these events; hence indicating seven 'coincidences' when an intervention event was followed by improvements in school attendance. Therefore, a strong causal link can be made between the intervention programme and the progress made in school attendance in this particular case.

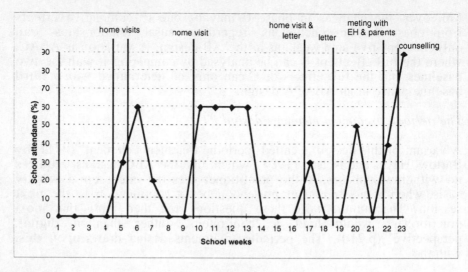

Figure 2.9   EH's school attendance (a PTD design)
Source: *Kazi, Craven and Wilson (1995)*

Multiple-baseline designs

Multiple-baseline designs are amongst the more sophisticated variations available that do not require a withdrawal phase. The multiple-baseline design enables researchers to draw causal inferences regarding the relationship between a specific treatment intervention and its effect on a client's target problem. The three types of multiple-baseline designs measure outcomes across clients, across settings, and across client's multiple target problems (Thyer 1993, p.110). Nelsen (1988) explains that these designs incorporate the basic AB design format as the AB design is replicated by applying the same intervention to more than one target problem, client or setting.

Bloom and Fischer (1982) describe the multiple-baseline design across clients as one 'in which the same practitioner applies the same intervention sequentially to two or more persons/groups who exhibit the same problems in the same settings' (p.334). Nelsen (1988), however, suggests that a 'multiple baseline study across client systems can sometimes be carried out by several practitioners working together, considerably reducing the workload for any one' (p.374). According to Thyer (1993), the requisites for this design include two or more clients with the same target problem, an intervention to be sequentially applied with each client, and a reliable and valid dependent variable. Nelsen (1988, p. 374) illustrates the design across clients with three single-parent clients all of whom wished to be more assertive with their children. All three presented self-report data on the percentage of times they actually had been appropriately assertive with their children (percentiles were used as the absolute number of positive responses would have varied according to the opportunities available for each parent). The intervention programme consisted of assertiveness training which was applied to all three clients; the same intervention was applied sequentially to each client, with the same positive results sequentially apparent in each case. According to Bloom and Fischer 1982 (pp. 329-343), the controlled application of the intervention and the predicted sequential effect become the basis for an inference that the practitioner's efforts are causes for the observed change. Thyer (1993) also argues that the improvements observed following the sequential administration of the intervention 'exclude most plausible threats to internal validity' (p.112). However, both Thyer (1993) and Kazdin (1982) point that an important condition for determining causal relationships with multiple-baseline designs is that the clients involved must not be influenced by each other.

The design across settings can be used to evaluate the effectiveness of an intervention in improving a single client's target problem observed in different settings. For example, a child's disruptiveness can be monitored at home, at school and with peers (Nelsen, 1988). The same intervention can be applied to each setting sequentially, and if the improvements can be observed at the onset of the intervention in each setting, similar inferences can be made regarding the effectiveness of the intervention as with the design across clients. Illustrations of this design can be found in Thyer (1993), Bloom and Fischer (1982), and several other texts named above.

The multiple-baseline design across target problems can be used to monitor two or more target problems experienced by the same client, evaluating the effectiveness of the same intervention aimed at improving each of the target problems. This design is illustrated in Thyer (1993, p. 115), using an example of a seven-year-old girl experiencing four problems in her home, namely hitting siblings, name-calling and swearing, and lateness to bed. The intervention included a parent training programme in child management techniques which the parents then systematically applied to each target problem in succession. The results were positive each time the intervention was applied, in succession. Inferences could be drawn with confidence that the intervention was responsible for the change.

Bloom and Fischer (1982) describe the strengths and limitations of the multiple-baseline designs. The strengths include their flexibility, e.g. dealing with multiple problems sequentially according to priority; the stronger causal inferences that can be drawn without withdrawal phases; and testing the generalisability of interventions across clients.

Limitations include the requirement of two or more baselines which may not be possible in some practice circumstances; the sequential use of the intervention which may be problematic in the designs across target problems as there may be an unknown effect of the order in which they are chosen (and random choice may not be possible if they are of equal importance); and the use of one specific intervention which may be problematic if more than one intervention is required to deal with more than one problem/client/setting.

Finally, a key problem is the degree of independence of the baselines as the introduction of the intervention on one baseline may affect the other(s). In the design across clients, if the clients are not influenced by each other, this problem may not arise; but in the intervention with the single client, care must be taken to select problems that appear to be relatively distinct from each other (Bloom and Fischer, 1982). Another recommendation from the authors is the use of more than two baselines, as the chances then are greater that there may be at least two baselines that are not interdependent. As a last resort, an experimental removal may be needed on one of the baselines if the interdependence cannot be minimised.

Requirements for the application of single-case designs

The following is an outline of the requirements for the application of single-case designs, based on some key published texts (Bloom and Fischer 1982; Kazdin 1982; Nelsen 1988; Sheldon 1982b, 1983; Barlow and Hersen, 1984; Bloom, Fischer and Orme 1995).

Specify the target problem (dependent variable)

The first step is to identify the target problem. Its description must be clear and not too vague or global. The investigator must develop an operational definition that will allow the client's problem (or concern) to be objectively measured. Problems selected must be those to which measurable indicators can be assigned.

Measure the problem

The second step is to collect repeated information on the target problem over regular periods of time to see whether any changes take place. Continuous assessment over time is used as a basis for drawing inferences about intervention effects. The measurements must be regular and systematic, and must be standardised across all phases in the design.

A wide range of measuring tools are available, e.g. self-reports or reports from observers using standardised measuring instruments   such as questionnaires and rating scales. Latterly, qualitative measures are also acceptable (Bloom, Fischer and Orme 1995). The operations involved in obtaining measurements must be clearly specified, observable, and replicable in all respects. In all cases, there should be checks on the reliability and validity of the measurement procedures used.

The design and phases

As discussed above, an almost infinite range of design options are available. The selection of an appropriate design depends on the number of clients to be involved in the evaluation, the availability of concurrent or reconstructed baseline data, the number of target problems to be dealt with, the number of interventions to be used with each target problem, and whether withdrawal phases (return to baseline) can be introduced.

Length of phases should allow sufficient data points to provide a clear and stable description of the events at the time. The lengths should be equal wherever possible, allowing external and internal factors to equally influence behaviours in baseline and intervention phases. However, even if the phase lengths are not equal, marked changes with the onset of each phase can still provide clues regarding causality. Designs do not have to be used in a mechanical way; procedures can be changed and reconstructed if necessary, as long as due care is given to their subsequent interpretation.

Intervention (independent variable)

Usually, a particular treatment interview takes place and then intervention phase B begins. It is possible to use several interventions at the same time, or even start one afterwards, as long as they are carefully monitored and reported. However, a cardinal rule of experimental single-case research is to change one variable at a time when proceeding from one phase to the next. Evaluating different interventions can introduce ambiguity, unless a particular intervention programme is found to be totally ineffectual, i.e., the baseline remains the same, and another intervention programme is introduced.

Whenever possible, relatively short periods are advocated, as long ones might allow enough time for the establishment of new conditioned reinforcers. Interventions may involve antecedent and consequent events delivered by persons in contact with the client. It is useful to observe both the responses of the client and the events delivered by others that constitute the intervention. It is important to clearly define the intervention to be used and to differentiate between the formal intervention period and periods when formal intervention programme is not established, e.g. assessment/baseline phase. Records should include the form and content of any intervention used, the frequency of its use and the context in which it is used.

Analysis of data

Single-case designs rely heavily on visual analysis---charts for easy visual inspection of changes in data patterns (level of data, trends, slope and so on). Simple statistics are also used particularly when visual analysis alone is found to be insufficient and the statistical significance is to be tested. Graphs are probably the best method as they provides information at a glance, and patterns and trends show up quite readily. Computer programmes are also available for analysis (Bloom, Fischer and Orme 1995).

The clinical and statistical significance of the findings should be discussed. Intervening variables cannot be completely eliminated, but the application of experimental designs and basic statistics hopefully can help to control variability and search for functional relations between dependent and independent variables.

However, in practice, social workers may be required to make accommodations either for ethical or procedural reasons. According to most texts, deviations from some of the above requirements during the earlier stages are acceptable, but increased rigour is recommended at later stages. Once technical procedures and major parametric concerns have been dealt with satisfactorily, a more rigorous pursuit of scientific rigour would be expected. In short, as in any scientific endeavour, as increased knowledge accrues the level of experimental sophistication should reflect its concurrent growth (Hersen and Barlow 1976, pp. 102-103).

Changes in the requirements

In the course of application, a number of changes have taken place in the requirements of single-case designs---changes which have helped to enhance the utility of this methodology in practice. The earlier emphasis was on the use of single-case designs to establish a causal link between the intervention and its effects. Therefore, most of the authors of the texts referred to in this chapter tended to suggest that, whilst designs such as B and AB could be used in the earlier stages of evaluation, practitioners should move up in a hierarchy of designs striving to achieve the experimental ABAB design at the top end of this hierarchy. The implication was that practitioners would plan at the outset which design would be used, including the withdrawal of the intervention in order to establish a causal link. They also emphasised the need to use reliable measures---usually standardised measures with proven reliability such as in Corcoran and Fischer (1987). Whilst emphasising the ideal requirements, these authors would at the same time acknowledge the need for flexibility, and the paramouncy of practice needs rather than research needs; but the message was clear: go for the ideal if you can.

These emphases may in part account for why single-case designs were not used extensively in the earlier stages. For example, there is still a tendency to define single-case designs in terms of these more rigorous requirements, such as in Shaw (1998) who argues that single-case designs are incompatible with most social work practice. Having read the requirements and the range of designs available, the reader will be apprehensive and probably conclude that single-case evaluation is not for him/her. Do not despair! Although these requirements address the needs of the most experimental-conscious practitioner, they certainly do not have to be followed by those whose evaluation perspectives are not inclined in this direction. And yet you could still use single-case designs within such perspectives. This is because, in the course of application, the emphases in the definitions and requirements have changed along with the needs of practice.

As indicated in Chapter 1, the definition of single-case designs in *Encyclopaedia of Social Work* no longer emphasises the experimental question or the need to establish a causal link (Blythe 1995). In the course of application, and particularly in the 1990s, authors who have experience of extensive promotion of single-case designs in practice (Blythe and Rodgers 1993, Kazi 1998) have contributed to this change of emphasis which has enhanced the utility of single-case designs in practice. The main emphasis is on the use of single-case designs to systematically track client progress or to determine the extent to which the target problem has changed.

The minimum requirements are the specification and operationalising of target problems, and the use of appropriate measures. The nature of the design used then unfolds with practice. For example, the designs illustrated in this chapter from the work of Kirklees Education Social Workers were not planned in advance. Once the measure was identified and used repeatedly, the nature of the design and the use of baselines or the withdrawals of intervention all fell into place naturally as practice unfolded. In all cases, the evaluative question was addressed; i.e., whether progress was made or not. In some cases where baselines and withdrawal phases unfolded, it was possible to establish a causal link between the intervention and the progress, but that was almost in passing.

As for the use of measures, whilst practitioners were encouraged to try standardised measures where appropriate, they were also helped in the construction of their own measures---measures that they were able to design for specific purposes. They were encouraged to enhance the reliability of such measures through simple steps e.g. anchoring rating scales with as precise definitions as possible, and administering the measures in the same way each time (e.g. as a group activity in the adult rehabilitation unit---see Chapter 5). These shifts in the requirements of rigour are examined in more detail in the studies reported in the foregoing chapters.

3 Examples of Research in Education Social Work

This chapter provides exemplars from school based social work. These exemplars are from the first agency-wide study undertaken in 1993, as well as subsequent studies within the same agency to evaluate specific truancy and behaviour projects. The 1993 effectiveness study was this author's first, based at Kirklees Education Social Work Service, i.e., an agency providing social work services to school pupils and their families within Kirklees Metropolitan Council---a local authority in Yorkshire, England. The agency's services are aimed at school children, their families and teachers, to help resolve both home- and school-based problems. Funded by the local authority, this study's central aim was to enable social workers to become practitioner-evaluators, using single-case designs on an agency-wide basis.

Through a training programme, the methodology was made available to all practitioners in the social work agency, together with organisational and informational supports to encourage implementation by practitioners. In the event, 21 social workers used single-case evaluation in 83 cases, as reported in Kazi and Wilson (1993, 1996 and 1996a). At the time of writing, single-case evaluation has been incorporated into the agency's working procedures, particularly in the evaluation of specific truancy and disaffection projects.

The work setting of the participating social workers

Blyth, Kazi and Milner (1994) describe the nature of social work services in school settings in England and Wales. The introduction of market forces within the education system has led to increased demands on support services to identify their aims and objectives and to demonstrate their effectiveness. According to a 1992 report of the Service Manager Joe Wilson, the Kirklees Education Social Work Service provides a social work service in an education (school) setting, the

43

main aim of which is to assist children to benefit from the educational opportunities available to them and help children, families and schools to deal with problems which may be preventing the children from realising their full potential. The agency is part of a wide range of community provision and collaborates with other helping agencies in offering services to children and families, such as schools, social services, health, police, probation services and voluntary agencies.

The services provided are reported to include the following areas of work:

- promoting equal opportunities in access to education;

- social work, counselling, family and groupwork services to children, family and schools;

- dealing with school attendance problems;

- advise and provision of education welfare benefits such as free school meals and clothing;

- child protection, including joint work with other agencies and the training of teachers;

- assisting with assessment and provision for special educational needs;

- youth justice, including participation in police cautioning procedures, the preparation of court reports and other statutory duties; and

- dealing with behaviour problems and exclusions from school.

In undertaking the above tasks, it is reported that the social workers also seek to:

- enable service users to participate in decision-making processes;

- positively promote service users' own capabilities;

- challenge and confront personal, institutional and cultural racism and other forms of discrimination;

- promote effective communication between children, families and schools;

- show respect and regard for others in ability, age and culture appropriate ways.

At the time of the study, 15 out of the 29 practitioners were qualified social workers, and another 4 were attending a qualifying sandwich course during 50% of their working week. In addition, there were social workers in the School Psychological Service providing specialist support for children and families with problems of behaviour and other family problems, including the provision of child and family guidance clinics. Although not formally a part of the agency, these social workers had very close links with the Kirklees Education Social Work Service and fully participated in its training programmes.

Objectives of the study

The objectives in the use of this methodology were three-fold: 1) to enable practitioners to ascertain whether there were changes in their client's identified target problems; 2) to ascertain the extent to which the services they provided to the clients were responsible for those changes; and 3) to identify a methodology that could continue to be used by practitioners even after the study had ceased, hence providing potential long term benefits. The study was designed to generate empirical data in order to evaluate the relevance and effectiveness of direct client services---services in which many outcomes are usually deemed to be unmeasurable (England 1986).

Although the study was funded by the local authority for one year in the 1992-1993 financial year, it remained in existence from April 1992 to September 1993. The main reason for this extension was because it took longer than anticipated to introduce, train and encourage practitioners to use the methodology and to generate sufficient data to achieve the above aims and objectives of the study. The study was based in the Kirklees Education Social Work Service as well as Child Guidance, involving all the social workers working in an education (or school) setting. These practitioners showed a great deal of enthusiasm for the study. All the training and research sessions were well-attended at both Service and Team levels, and in the event data including 94 cases was generated (92 from Kirklees Education Social Work Service and 2 from Child Guidance).

Strategy for application of single-case evaluation

In its initial phases, the study concentrated on the implementation of

Robinson, Bronson and Blythe's (1988) recommendations to encourage a wider use of single-case evaluation. First, the agency managers acknowledged that the findings from these evaluations would not be used in personnel decisions as a method of judging or comparing practitioners. Second, in order to bridge the gap between research and practice, the utility of single-case evaluation was demonstrated with a number of practice methods used by a forward group of practitioners. Initially, four social workers took the lead in volunteering to apply the designs in their work. A training session was held for all staff which provided the opportunity to the four social workers to disseminate their experiences to the others. Third, the Kirklees Education Social Work Service management ensured that appropriate time and resources were made available for all practitioners who wanted to participate in this study. Fourth, regular training sessions were held which were open to all practitioners and follow-up meetings and workshops were held individually with each of the agency's three teams at their bases. On-going consultancy was also provided on demand. Fifth, the trainers fostered positive attitudes with intensive, practical assistance to practitioners at the initial stages, highlighting the benefits for both practitioners and their clients. Sixth, the practitioners themselves actively participated in designing the data forms and the measuring formats required for the application of single-case evaluation designs in their practice. The ownership of the design and measures was theirs, prepared in consultation with the trainers (namely the author and the service manager). Finally, the trainers avoided jargon and academic language as far as was possible, and the use of complicated statistics [e.g. standard error of measurement and celeration line in Kazdin (1982)] was also avoided.

In their study of social workers in the United States, Penka and Kirk (1991) found that 'many social workers who engage in some clinical evaluation do not recognise the extent to which they are engaging in it or do not realise how a few additional activities (for example the use of objective measures) could put their work in the realm of practice research'. The methodology used in this study consisted of these 'few additional activities' referred to above (Sheldon 1983, Bloom and Fischer 1982). In this study, the earlier attempts were to encourage practitioners to use single-case designs with withdrawal phases that could enable a causal link to be inferred between the intervention and its effects. However, on the basis of the experience of the advance group of practitioners who attempted to use the designs first, the emphasis was changed and placed firmly on the pre-requisites namely programme clarification and measurement techniques, rather than on the research designs, for two reasons. First, it was accepted that evaluative research was secondary to the practice itself, i.e., the research designs were applied 'not as a master of practice but as a guide to practice' (Bloom and Fischer 1982). Second, as Sheldon (1984) found in his experience of using and teaching these research designs, the main difficulties of this approach 'lie not in persuading clients to co-operate, not in the production of graphs, but in the early stages of choosing and defining the parameters to be measured'. With these considerations in mind, this study's research strategy was to train practitioners in the evaluation process of breaking down global target problems into measurable, component parts (or indicators), selecting appropriate measures, and then proceeding with their practice. The type of single-case research design used would then fall into place naturally, depending on the needs of practice.

Bloom and Fischer (1982) describe this process of operationalising target problems or goals. For example, absenteeism from school could be measured in terms of days per week, being overweight could be measured in terms of weight against height and weight norms, bed-wetting could be measured in terms of number of times per week. The form devised for collection of data from practitioners for this study was based on the need to operationalise target problems, hence starting from the reasons for referral, to a description of the global problems, and then finally describing the specific components.

The next step in this process of evaluation is to identify appropriate measures for the selected component parts of the target problem that are to be changed with social work intervention. Both quantitative and qualitative measures were used in this study, in keeping with Bostwick and Kyte (1993)'s definition of measurement and Blythe and Tripodi (1989)'s levels of measurement. The measures provided for practitioners participating in this study consisted of a comprehensive range which could be applied to any client target problem that the participating social workers were likely to come across. First, copies of Corcoran and Fischer (1987) were supplied which include 125 standardised measuring instruments over a wide range of target problems. Second, formats were constructed to provide a range of flexible instruments, based on descriptions from Bloom and Fischer (1982) and Barlow, Hayes and Nelson (1984) and the needs of practitioners ascertained in a series of research meetings. The practitioners themselves fully participated in the construction of these measuring instruments. These formats were then circulated to all practitioners together with fictitious examples to illustrate possible uses of each of the formats.

The formats included a spot checking behaviour chart to facilitate the recording of observations at specific times, an attendance bar chart to record school attendance as a percentage of the total possible attendance per school week, global self-anchored scales for clients to record their feelings and attitudes retrospectively over a period of time, rating and self-anchored scales which could be used for measurement at specific periods of time for a variety of problems, a satisfaction scale to measure feelings in three categories (unhappy, neutral and happy) using facial expressions, and an essentially qualitative descriptive measure--the ABC chart to record antecedents, behaviours and consequences in a sequence over time (a client log as described in Bloom and Fischer 1982).

The research designs used in this study are drawn from the range of single-case designs described in the published texts and as described in Chapter 2. However, the strategy of this study was to concentrate on training social workers in the basic requirements of single-case evaluation, namely the operationalisation of target problems and the selection of appropriate measuring instruments. The exact single-case design used was to be determined by the needs of practice. A number of texts describe the use of statistics in the analysis of data (e.g. Kazdin 1982); however, in the experience of the author in teaching on a qualifying social work course, students and practitioners tend to be discouraged from using these designs by what appear to be complicated statistical analyses. Mutschler (1984) also found that although training was provided to the six social workers participating in her study, none of them actually used the statistical assessment techniques. Therefore, in this study, only the basic statistics were used, e.g. tables, scattergrams and line charts, with a heavy reliance on visual analysis.

The Kirklees study's basic strategy was to concentrate on the designs' prerequisites and enable the exact nature of the designs to be determined by practice considerations (and therefore the needs of the clients) rather than research considerations. Training was provided for practitioners in the evaluation process of breaking down global target problems into measurable, component parts (or indicators), selecting appropriate measures, and then proceeding with practice. Although the social work practitioners were trained on the range of single-case designs available, the study's strategy was that, once the prerequisites were applied, the exact nature of the design would fall into place as the practice unfolded. This position has since been corroborated by the methodological shifts identified by Blythe and Rodgers (1993), namely the 'realisation that we do not select a design at the outset of work with a client. Rather, designs are determined as practice evolves' (Blythe and Rodgers 1993, p. 106).

The social workers began with the use of standardised measures from Corcoran and Fischer (1987) and Bloom and Fischer (1982). They concluded that, although some of these measures were useful, they needed to construct their own measures for the range of client problems they were addressing. As a result, the social workers themselves created formats for measuring school attendance, behaviour, feelings and attitudes---measures which were academically acceptable and at the same time flexible enough to be used with most of the target problems addressed in their practice. This is, again, in keeping with the methodological shifts identified by Blythe and Rodgers (1993)---the realisation that measures other than those of proven reliability could be constructed.

The training sessions concentrated on the application of single-case evaluation rather than its description. The participating social workers selected real cases from their caseload and brought them for consideration to these sessions. The target problems were made specific and a selection of appropriate measures were identified. Armed with these ideas, the social worker would use one or two of these in collaboration with the client, and then report on progress in future training sessions. In a number of cases, social workers used measures which were not appropriate either because the target problems were not identified correctly or because the clients did not consider them to be relevant. These difficulties were overcome with the construction of a number of measuring instruments to enable the social workers to be better prepared and to make selections with the clients. The social workers shared these experiences and learnt from them.

The selection of cases for the study

Twenty one social workers in the employment of Kirklees Metropolitan Council submitted data from their practice for this evaluation research study. From this total, 20 were social workers working in Kirklees Education Social Work Service, and one was a social worker with Child and Family Guidance section of the School Psychological Service. Kirklees Education Social Work Service includes a total of 29 social work practitioners (not counting the managers) working in an education setting. All of these practitioners participated in the study by attending the various training and research meetings held both at their work places and at the University of Huddersfield. In the event, 69% of these social workers provided data for this study. The School Psychological Service includes a total of three social workers, and one of these three submitted data. It should be noted that during the period of the study, substantial reductions were made in the budget of Kirklees Education Social Work Service which included reductions in the number of social workers employed, hence adversely affecting staff morale at that time.

Altogether, data involving 94 cases was included in this study from the 1992/93 school academic year. Following one year of preparation (April 1992 to April 1993), practitioners who had not yet provided any data for analysis were asked to select the first five or six referrals received from April 1993 onwards. Apart from this guidance, the practitioners themselves selected the cases from their workloads---cases in which they felt they could apply the single-case evaluation methodology introduced to them. The participating practitioners were enabled and encouraged to sample the use of this methodology in an unobtrusive way in the course of their daily practice. Therefore, in the sample of cases included in this study, there was no random method of selection, and the conclusions that can be drawn from the findings of this study relate only to the effectiveness of the practitioners in these particular cases. Of the 94 cases considered in this study, 92 were received from Kirklees Education Social Work Service and the remaining 2 from the School Psychological Service (Child Guidance). The Education Social Work Service is reported to have received approximately 3,800 referrals in the school year 1992/93, and therefore the cases included in this study represented only 2.4% of the total number of cases received by that service. No comparable data are available from the social workers in the School Psychological Service as they tend to report to their managers by the number of service days rather than the number of total cases. Out of the 94 cases submitted by practitioners, 8 could not be analysed in this study as no measures were used, and a further 3 included measures which were either incomplete or not clearly presented. Therefore, only 83 of these cases were analysed in this study.

The foregoing includes illustrations of some of these cases, to reflect the evidence-based approach of operationalising target problems and assigning outcome measures. These examples are in addition to others already included in Chapter 2 as examples of particular types of single-case designs.

Some case examples

Case 1---AC

At the request of her mother, AC---a primary school girl aged eight years---was referred to the social worker for help with management of behaviour at home. AC was described as aggressive and destructive. In order to make these global descriptions more precise, the social worker asked both parents to log all significant incidents of bad behaviour, using a chart to log not only the behaviours but also the antecedents and consequences wherever possible (hence called 'ABC' chart). At the same time, an intervention programme consisting of advice and support for both parents was initiated to enhance their skills for managing AC's behaviour.

Client: AC   **Observer: Parents**

DATE	WHAT HAPPENED BEFORE	BEHAVIOUR	WHAT HAPPENED AFTER
8/5 10.00 am	Asked AC to fetch extension and unroll it	Banged on floor,trying to break it	Told to put it down and leave it
		Ran into the house & slammed the door, calling mother "silly cow"	Sent to bed for 1/2 hour
12/5 4.30 pm	Asked to go to friend's house and told no	Told me she was going anyway	Told to stay in garden or to go to bed
14/5 8.25 pm		Set alarm off	Sent to bed
15/6 5.45 pm	Asked to go to friend's house and told no	Being cheeky	Ignored her

Figure 3.1   Excerpts from the 'ABC' chart kept by AC's parents
Source: *Kazi (1996a)*

Figure 3.1 illustrates some excerpts from the 'ABC' chart, essentially a qualitative measure used by AC's parents. The data from this measure is then quantified in Figure 3.2, as the number of days per week when bad behaviour did not take place.

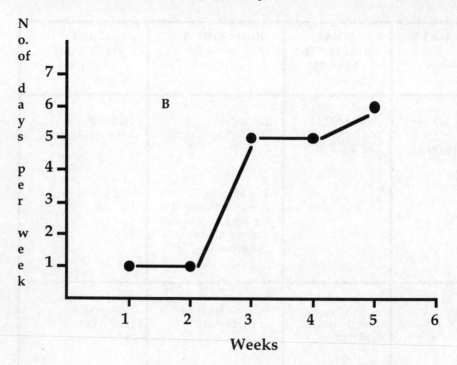

Figure 3.2 **Number of days per week when bad behaviour did not occur**

Source: *Kazi (1996a)*

Figure 3.2 illustrates a 'B' design, i.e., no baseline measurements were available and the target problem was measured during the intervention programme. This design is at the bottom end of the experimental continuum. The only inference that can be drawn is that behaviour improved in the course of the six weeks. No further conclusions can be drawn with regard to the extent to which the intervention programme itself was responsible for the changes observed. Nevertheless, the 'B' design can provide useful information on progress to both the worker and the client. This case is an example of how qualitative and quantitative data can be combined to provide such information.

Case 2---GL

GL, aged 13 years, attends a local high school. Following a pattern of absenteeism from school, the head teacher referred his case to the social worker. The social worker found that most of the absences had taken place following the diagnosis of asthma by the family's doctor. The social worker's intervention was to liaise with the doctor and other medical staff, and to arrive at an understanding with both GL and his parents regarding the circumstances when he could or could not attend school, accepting that GL's attendance may not be 100% due to his condition. The measure used was the school attendance register, marked twice a day by the teacher.

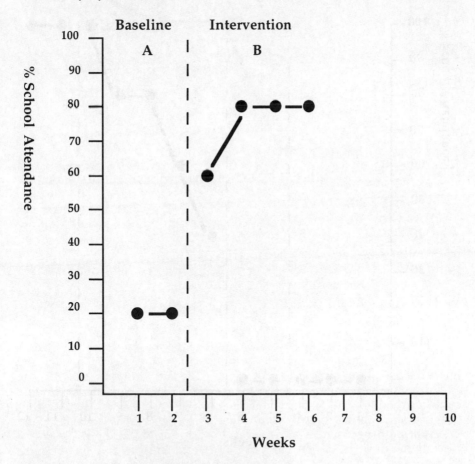

Figure 3.3   **GL's school attendance**
Source: *Kazi and Wilson (1996)*

Figure 3.3 illustrates the results. An immediate improvement took place at the onset of the intervention, and then GL's attendance at school was stable for three weeks during the intervention. The 'evaluative' question (Thyer 1993) is adequately addressed, indicating clear progress in the target problem. Although Thyer states that the AB design cannot address the 'experimental' question, according to Bloom and Fischer (1982) an immediate change at the onset of the intervention can provide an indication that the intervention was probably responsible for the change.

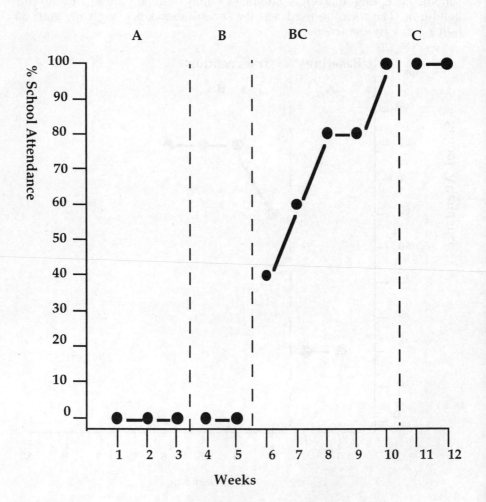

Figure 3.4   **JH's school attendance**
Source: *Kazi and Wilson (1996)*

Case 3---JH

JH, aged 15 years, attends a local high school. JH's attendance at school had dropped sharply in the previous four months, at the time when she began a relationship with a new boyfriend and left home to live with him. At the time this case was referred to the social worker, JH had returned home and her mother had requested help. The intervention programme was to effect a gradual introduction back to school and to arrange positive encouragement from teachers (C). The social worker also provided weekly counselling sessions for grandmother, mother, JH and boyfriend (B). The measures used were the school attendance register (Figure 3.4) and a self-anchored scale (Figure 3.5). The register plotted JH's attendance at school twice a day, and the self-anchored scale was used to determine mother's feelings about the relationship with her daughter on a five-point scale ranging from 'very bad relationship' (1) to 'very good relationship' (5).

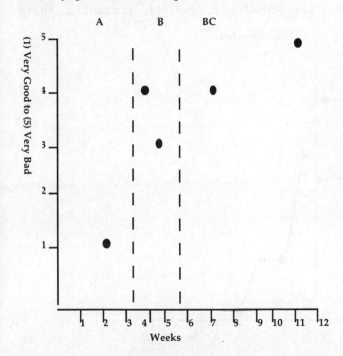

Figure 3.5   **Mother's feelings about relationship with JH on a five-point scale ranging from (1) 'very bad' to (5) 'very good'**

Source: *Kazi and Wilson (1996)*

Figure 3.4 illustrates an A-B-BC-C design which is similar to the AB design but includes more than one intervention phase. The retrospective baseline data is stable throughout at 0%. The onset of intervention B did not effect an improvement, and therefore could be considered part of the baseline (Bloom and Fischer, 1982). When the intervention B was combined with C, there was an immediate, sharp improvement which continued throughout the BC phase and remained stable in the C phase. The evaluative question is clearly answered---it can be concluded that there were dramatic, significant improvements in attendance from BC onwards. The trend in the data (stability at 0% in A and 100% in C) provides a strong hint that the intervention C (when preceded by B) was responsible for these improvements, although alternative explanations cannot be ruled out with confidence.

This design was replicated (with the exception of the C phase) across the other target problem---mother's feelings about her relationship with JH (Figure 3.5), which indicates that there was an immediate improvement at the onset of B, which then tapered off; and when BC was introduced, another immediate, sharp

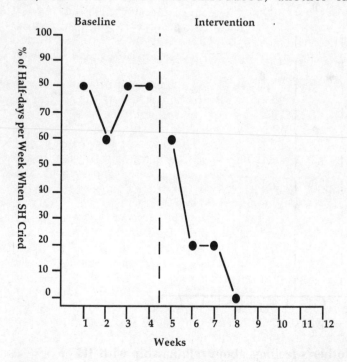

Figure 3.6   **Percentage of school half-days per week when SH cried in school**

Source: *Kazi and Wilson (1996)*

improvement took place which then continued throughout the phase BC. It can be concluded, therefore, that significant improvements were also achieved in this second dependent variable. Figure 3.5 indicates a strong hint that although B was not immediately effective in improving attendance, the intervention was probably responsible for the improvement in mother's feelings about the relationship with her daughter, and that when B was combined with C, this combination was probably responsible for effecting a still further improvement. As there are now two designs, both indicating that the intervention(s) led to improvements in two target problems, the causal inferences can be drawn with greater confidence (Barlow, Hayes and Nelsen 1984).

Case 4---SH

SH, aged 11 years, was referred to the social worker by a local high school as she was having great difficulty settling in the new school and was described as 'weepy'. SH cried often both in school and at night, to the extent that she was unable to sleep at night and was refusing to go to school. The parents were trying their best to resolve the situation, but felt worn down by her tears. The social worker's intervention programme consisted of a plan to enhance SH's importance in the school, combined with frequent counselling, involving both the social worker and relevant teachers.

The incidence of crying at school was measured as the percentage of school half-days per week when SH cried as reported by SH's form teacher (and also self-reported by SH). Baseline data was obtained retrospectively. Figure 3.6 illustrates an AB design. The data in the retrospective baseline A was fairly stable. The onset of the intervention programme brought an immediate, sharp improvement in the target problem of crying in school, and this trend of improvement was maintained throughout the intervention phase B, until the crying stopped in week 8. Follow-up contacts indicated that there was no crying in the following 6 weeks. The same intervention programme was applied to the dependent variable of crying at home in the school weeks 6 and 7. Figure 3.7 represents a B design which indicates significant improvements were made in this period, completely removing the incidence of crying at home in the second week.

The Hare Self-Esteem Scale (HSS) is a 30-item instrument designed for the purpose of measuring self-esteem in children 10 years old or above. It consists of three 10-item subscales that are arena specific (peer, home and school). Reliability is reported to be .74 and concurrent validity .83 for the general scale. No cutting score is suggested, and higher scores indicate higher self-esteem (Corcoran and Fischer, 1987). The results of the HSS applied at the start of the intervention and at a follow-up after the intervention (Figure 3.8) indicate stable levels of self-esteem in the comparison between these two points. There were no significant changes in self-esteem, which suggests that there may have been no connection between the incidence of crying and the level of self-esteem.

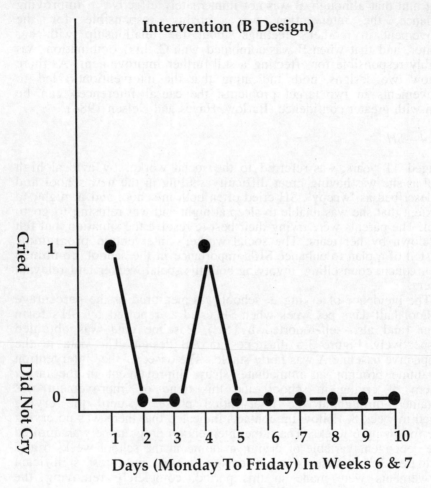

Figure 3.7 **School days when SH cried at night in weeks 6 and 7**
(1 = cried; 0 = did not cry)

Source: *Kazi and Wilson (1996)*

From the results of the data in relation to the above three dependent variables, it can be concluded that there were significant improvements in the incidence of crying both at school and at home during the intervention period, and that information obtained in a follow-up suggested that these improvements continued after the intervention ceased. The trend in the data in Figure 3.6 also provides a strong hint that the intervention programme was responsible for the improvement in the incidence of crying at school, although alternative explanations cannot be ruled out.

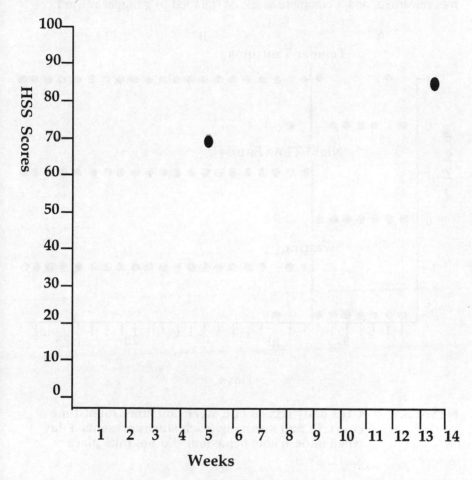

Figure 3.8   SH's Hare Self-Esteem (HSS) scores
Source: Kazi and Wilson (1996)

Case 5---CH

CH, aged 7 years, was referred by her mother for problems of behaviour, namely swearing, night-time enuresis and temper tantrums.

The aims agreed by the social worker were to develop mother's parenting skills, improve parent-child relationships, and to improve CH's behaviour. The intervention programme consisted of behaviour modification---each of the behaviours was recorded by the parent, and a star awarded on the days when the behaviour did not occur. Each star was rewarded, and a complete week of stars led to a bigger reward.

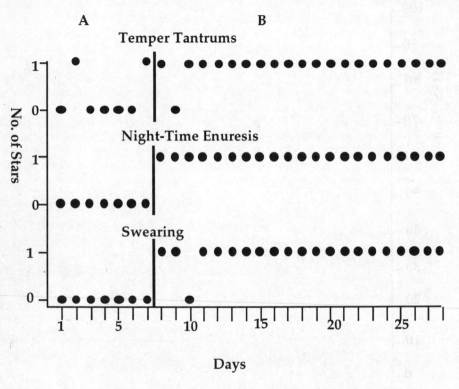

Figure 3.9 **CH's daily record of temper tantrums, night-time enuresis, and swearing (each star represents a day when undesirable behaviour did not take place**

Source: *Kazi (1996a)*

In this example, the mother's concerns about CH's behaviour were operationalised into three key behaviours, and the same intervention programme was used across the three target problems. Figure 3.9 illustrates three AB designs, each indicating an immediate, sharp improvement at the onset of intervention. Taken together, this is an experimental design which indicates not only that the target problems improved, but also that the intervention programme was responsible for the changes (Barlow and Hersen 1984). It is significant that the data used is in fact classificatory data, on the interface between quantitative and qualitative data.

CASE 6---CN

CN, a 19-year old high school pupil, was referred by the head of year due to concerns over living accommodation. CN was living in rented property several miles way from the school and having to work part time to pay her rent, with school work suffering at a time when the pre-university 'A' level exams were approaching. CN herself was very worried and unhappy over the situation.

The intervention programme was to arrange interviews with a housing association and Citizens Advice Bureau, to support CN's application for housing and to obtain financial help from charities. In the event, financial help was obtained from the charity Round Table for four months to cover her for the period of study, and CN was rehoused in the fifth month of the intervention. The measure used was a Satisfaction Scale, monitoring CN's feelings about the progress made every month, with the results illustrated in Figure 3.10.

Month 1	unhappy
Month 2	unhappy
Month 3	neutral........Financial help obtained at this point
Month 4	neutral
Month 5	happy....................Rehoused at this point.

Figure 3.10   CN's feelings about the progress made every month

Figure 3.10 shows a clear trend from unhappy to neutral at the point when financial help was obtained, and then from neutral to happy when she was finally rehoused. According to the principle of unlikely successive coincidences (Thyer 1993), if the design illustrated in this case can be seen to be Periodic Treatment Element Design (PTD--described in Chapter 2), the two coincidences of change in CN's feelings at the points of intervention allow an inference, although with a low degree of confidence, that the social worker's intervention was responsible for the improvement. However, as the design extends over five months, and as other agencies were involved (namely the source of financial help and the housing association), alternative explanations can be plausible. Moreover, the only measure used was the Satisfaction

Scale, with a low reliability due to possible random errors in the measurement process as discussed later in this Chapter. All that can be said with certainty is that the objectives of the intervention were realised in the five month period.

Case 7---PW

PW, a 10-year old junior school pupil, was referred by the head teacher for intermittent absenteeism. It appeared that the parent allowed the child to have several days off at a time for minor illnesses. The intervention was to work with the parent to increase her awareness of the actual extent of absences and to monitor future attendance with her to achieve improvements. The measure used was the school attendance register, and the results were as illustrated in Figure 3.11.

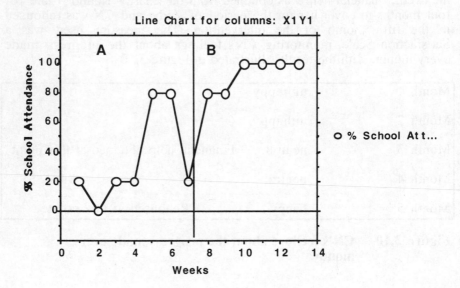

Figure 3.11   PW's school attendance (replicated AB design)

Figure 3.11 illustrates an AB design that clearly shows an improvement. The immediate, sharp improvement in school attendance at the onset of the intervention which then remains stable at 100% allows an inference that the intervention was the probable cause of this improvement. However, alternative explanations such as history cannot be ruled out, particularly as the trend in the baseline data was also towards improvement--unless this AB design is replicated across clients, as it was in this case (see discussion of Case 9 in the foregoing).

Case 8---JM

JM, a 12-year old high school pupil, was referred by the head tutor of his year group due to absenteeism and lack of contact from home. JM's parents had split up and he had been living with his father; but JM's father died a year ago, and since then he has been in the care of an aunt and grandparents. The intervention was to establish links with the caring relatives and to seek their co-operation to monitor attendance with school and social worker, and to provide encouragement for JM, in order to achieve improvements. The measure used was the attendance register, with the results illustrated in Figure 3.12.

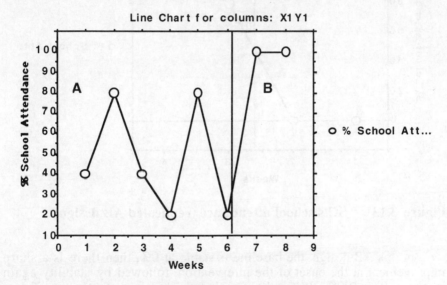

Figure 3.12   JM's school attendance (replicated AB design)

Figure 3.12 illustrates an AB design, showing clear improvement in attendance during the intervention phase B. The improvement is immediate and dramatic, achieving 100% in two weeks. However, only a hint of the causal inference can be made, as data during phase A is not stable, and there are only two measurement points in phase B. Nevertheless, the causal inference was further strengthened with replication of the design across clients (see discussion for Case 9).

Case 9---SC

SC, a 12-year old pupil at a high school, was referred by the head of year for unauthorised absences. He had been absent the week before and the week after half-term holidays with no contact from parents. The intervention was to establish contact with parents, to monitor attendance with them and to encourage SC. The measure used was the attendance register, with the results as illustrated in Figure 3.13.

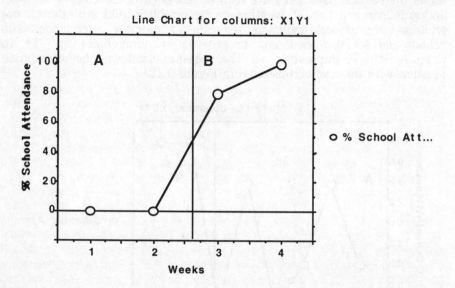

Figure 3.13   SC's school attendance (replicated AB design)

In this AB design, the baseline is stable at 0%, then there is a sharp improvement at the onset of the intervention, followed by stability again in phase B at 100%. It can be concluded, therefore, that a significant improvement in attendance had been achieved, and the intervention was probably responsible for this improvement. However, the causal inference in this one case can only be weak, unless this design is replicated across other clients.

The same practitioner used the same intervention in cases 7,8,9, as well as a fourth one (that also indicated improvements in the intervention phase), using AB designs that indicated improvements in the same target problem of school attendance across four clients. Therefore, these four AB designs can be considered to be directly replicated, and in this way they become experimental (Barlow, Hayes and Nelsen 1984). Taken together, it can be concluded with a greater degree of confidence that the intervention was indeed responsible for the improvements in school attendance in each of the four cases, ruling out alternative explanations.

The target problems and outcome measures used

The term 'target problem' is defined as 'a measurable behaviour, feeling or cognition (idea, belief or attitude) that is either a problem in itself or symptomatic of some other problem' (Polster and Collins, 1993, p.244). The target problem is the dependent variable which the practitioner and/or client aims at for change purposes (Bloom and Fischer 1982).

Table 3.1 lists all the measures that were used in the sample. Altogether, a total of 136 target problems were operationalised in the 83 cases, with a number of cases identifying more than one target problem for each client. The most frequent included school attendance and other problems of behaviour both at home and in school. Other less frequent problems included those of a non-behavioural nature, such as parents' concerns regarding the running of the schools, self-esteem, the effects of a family tragedy, accommodation and finance, the effects of sexual abuse, and recurrent nightmares. For example, there were four cases where the target problems were parents' concerns regarding the schools. In one case, a parent felt that the teacher was not setting appropriate reading tasks for the child. The other three cases involved concerns regarding bullying, the implementation of a previously agreed school programme for a pupil diagnosed as dyslexic, and parental dissatisfaction with a teacher's handling of a pupil. The intervention programmes included improving contacts between the parents and the schools concerned, and implementation of agreed tasks. The measure selected in all four cases was a three-point scale to monitor the parent's satisfaction, using B designs.

In another case, a three-point satisfaction scale was used in a B design to monitor a teenager's feelings regarding her home situation following a sibling's death. In the case involving the effects of sexual abuse, five-point self-anchored scales were used in a pretest post-test design to monitor feelings of anger, guilt, powerlessness, worry, fear, feelings of responsibility for the abuse, and ability to make decisions. Such a wide range of cases indicates that single-case evaluation designs can also be applied to target problems other than those of behaviour. These cases are of particular significance as Robinson, Bronson and Blythe (1988) found that such applications of these designs were rare. Moreover, of the 125 intervention programmes used, 47 were described as counselling, indicating that single-case evaluation techniques can evaluate non-behavioural programmes. A limitation of this study was that intervention programmes were not described in the detail required for replication; nevertheless these 47 cases were described as counselling, ranging from structured weekly sessions to unstructured general advice and support for parents, none of which involved the direct management of behavioural change. The school attendance register was the most common measure, followed by rating and self-anchored scales, the Satisfaction Scale, frequency counts and standardised measures obtained from Corcoran and Fischer (1987). The Satisfaction Scale, frequency counts, rating and self-anchored scales, spot checks, and the ABC chart were among the formats devised in the course of the study, enabling the practitioners to use the formats as flexibly as required for a variety of potential target problems. The two qualitative indicators were created by the practitioners themselves.

Table 3.1   Target problems and measures used by agency social workers

Target Problems	N
School absenteeism	67
Behaviour problems	36
Relationship difficulties	11
Lack of assertiveness	4
Low self-esteem	4
Punctuality in attending school	3
Parental concerns of some nature	3
Communication difficulties	2
Family tragedy	1
Accommodation (housing)	1
Finances	1
Problem-solving difficulties	1
Nightmares	1
Sexual abuse	1

Outcome measures employed	N
School attendance register	59
Rating scale	21
Client satisfaction	18
Frequency count	15
Standardised instruments	11
Spot checks	7
ABC charts	3
Qualitative indicators	2

Source: Kazi and Wilson (1996)

A basic requirement of single-case designs is that the measures used must be valid and reliable as far as possible (Bloom, Fischer and Orme 1995). Therefore, the issues of reliability and validity were addressed in the training phase of the study. It was accepted that because of the complexities involved in both the variables being measured and the process of measurement, it was virtually impossible to construct a perfectly valid and reliable instrument. Nevertheless, an important part of the training programme was identification of the potential sources of error in measurement and strategies to control or lessen their impact.

Validity is described as the 'degree to which an instrument measures what it is supposed to' and reliability as the 'degree of accuracy or precision of a measuring instrument' (Bostwick and Kyte, 1993, p. 181). It is accepted that because of the complexities involved in both the variable being measured and the process of measurement, it is virtually impossible to construct a perfectly valid and reliable instrument. Nevertheless, the goal should be to identify potential sources of error in measurement and to 'control or lessen their impact' (ibid., p.193). There are two common types of errors, constant and random. Constant errors are those that arise from demographic characteristics, e.g. personal styles, intelligence, levels of literacy, cultural and social factors. Random errors are those factors that affect the measuring process in an inconsistent fashion. Where instruments are used as client self-reports, either by the school pupil or a parent, random errors may include tendencies in clients to give favourable impressions, to agree with statements regardless of content, and to give uncommon responses. In instruments that involve observation of behaviour by others (teachers, parents and practitioners), random errors may include the halo effect (tendency to be unduly influenced by one's general impressions), and errors of leniency, severity or convergence to the middle (tendency to rate too high, too low, or in the middle). Another problem is reactivity, e.g. when the act of recording in itself produces changes in behaviour.

Control for constant errors includes the use of socially neutral items and ensuring that the items in the instrument are clearly understood by the respondents. Random errors can be minimised if practitioners' instructions for use are clear and sufficiently neutral, respect for confidentiality and mutual trust is emphasised, and there is consistency in the use of the same instrument with the same client over time. Reactivity can be minimised with the use of unobtrusive measures. All of these errors can be minimised by using more than one measure and comparing the outcomes.

Amongst the measures used in the sample, the *school attendance register* (Table 3.1) is probably the most reliable and valid measure. The schools are required to maintain such registers by statute, and such registers can be used as evidence in court for some legal proceedings. The register is recorded twice a day, at the start of the morning and afternoon sessions. The measuring process at a given moment is essentially nominal, i.e. it is a nominal (classificatory), qualitative measure--either the pupil is present or he/she is absent. The recordings that are made then become ratio measurements, i.e., frequency counts which could be expressed as so many actual attendances out of a possible 10 per (five-day) school week. The measure is valid insofar as it measures attendance at the particular times of recording; however, particularly in secondary schools where pupils move from one classroom to another in the course of the sessions, it cannot be assumed that the pupil remained in school after the attendance was recorded. Another problem is lateness; schools have various arrangements, but the social workers reported that a common one is where a pupil not present at the time of registration signs in a late book and then the form teacher places an 'L' in the register.

Reliability is high if the teacher records attendance conscientiously without mistakes, and if the pupils adhere to the rules of signing in. As in other recordings of observed behaviour, reliability would be still higher if recordings were also made by another teacher and then the results were compared (i.e., inter-observer reliability), but that is in an ideal situation. As pointed out earlier, the errors in measurement can be minimised if more than one measure is used. In one case, spot checks were made by teachers in addition to the register recordings, and lesson report was used in two cases (described as an intervention, as it also involves praise for good behaviour in lessons). Nevertheless, attendance register recordings are accepted as a matter of routine, and are therefore unobtrusive. The nature of the recording is such that retrospective baselines can be constructed, as the process of recording remains the same throughout the school life.

With regard to *Spot checks* and *frequency counts* of behaviour, validity depends on a clear definition of behaviours that are to be recorded, and reliability depends on the extent to which this clarity is then maintained consistently. The main advantage in the use of these particular measures is that they reflected observation by significant others (parents, teachers and practitioners) in real life settings. The seven spot checks consisted of observations made by teachers of behaviour in school (3), observations made by a teacher of peer relationships in the playground (1), observations made by the social worker of classroom behaviour (1), observations made by a teacher after school attendance registration sessions to monitor actual attendance in lessons (1), and finally, a mother's observations of behaviour at home (1). Six of the fifteen frequency counts consisted of observations of school behaviours by teachers such as the number of positive responses to teacher's instructions, the number of violent incidents, occasions of inappropriate calling out in the classroom, and the incidence of crying in school. Six other frequency counts were made by parents of behaviour at home including incidences of refusal to obey reasonable parental instructions, swearing, enuresis, and temper tantrums. Three other frequency counts included self-monitoring by school students themselves, namely the incidence of nightmares, crying at night and efforts made to be friendly with peers.

The *Satisfaction Scale* is essentially a *self-anchored scale* with three points; its validity can be very high where there is clarity of what it is that is being measured in this way, but reliability depends on the respondent's consistency (and honesty in reporting) in anchoring the variable along the three points. The *Satisfaction Scale* has three facial expressions denoting unhappy-neutral-happy, and the respondent chooses one at the time of recording. It was felt that a recording of feelings would provide useful additional information particularly in the evaluation of intervention programmes implemented collaboratively with clients. This scale was used 18 times, out of which 9 were with pupils recording their feelings with regard to the progress made with the target problem, their feelings regarding their school and home situations, and their relationships. This scale was used a further 8 times with parents, expressing their feelings with the progress made so far in the target problem, feelings regarding their parenting, and feelings regarding school matters. On one occasion, this scale was also used by the social worker to determine clinical significance of changes in the target problem.

The *rating scales* are standardised across subjects, and again reliability depends on the degree to which the points are anchored. Therefore, measures involving the use of such scales cannot be precise and can provide only an indication of real changes in the variable. In a number of cases included in this study, such scales are used as additional measures, hence corroborating changes indicated by other instruments; however, in a small number of cases it is used as the only measure. For example, in one case, it was used as a measure of parent's satisfaction; this was a valid use of the instrument as the target problem was the parent's dissatisfaction with the school. In another, it was used to determine pupil's feelings following a tragic event, in which case the reliability and validity would be weaker due to random errors described earlier.

Standardised measures used were obtained from Corcoran and Fischer (1987), which records the reliability and validity of each measure. However, in the selection of such measures, content validity and utility are important factors. Often, the practitioner used these measures for assessment purposes rather than repeated application. The *ABC chart* (Figure 3.1) recording behaviours, antecedents and consequences) was used as a recording system with parents as observers--validity depends on the extent to which definitions of significant behaviours were clear, and reliability on the extent to which such definitions were applied consistently in the observation of the behaviour. The *ABC chart* is essentially a qualitative descriptive measure; in one case, it supplemented the information obtained from the use of other measures; in the case of AC illustrated above, a frequency count was derived from the information in the ABC chart. The parent was recording what she considered to be significant events involving the child's behaviour. Validity depends on the extent to which definitions of significant events were clear, and reliability on the extent to which such definitions were applied consistently in the observation of the behaviour. The qualitative descriptors were used in two cases; in each, the practitioner selected several performance indicators, and then at the end of the intervention identified (nominal) classificatory changes in these indicators. This information supplemented a B and an AB design which was also used in of these cases; in the second, a measure recording points awarded for good behaviour was also used, but it was lost by the respondent (another difficulty with self-report measures) and therefore not submitted.

Apart from the school attendance register, spot checks and frequency observations made by teachers and the social work practitioners, the bulk of the other measures used were of a self-report or self-monitoring nature, where the school students themselves or their parents were administering the measuring instruments. Such measures are generally subject to problems such as response bias or social desirability response set, although from the point of view of face validity it can be argued that the subjects are using and reporting on the measures they consider to be valid (Bloom and Fischer 1982). It is also argued that differences between self-rated performance scores and supervisor-rated performance scores may be due to differences in perception rather than accuracy (Alter and Evens 1990). In this research study, in the majority of cases self-report measures were used to supplement the other types of measures (school attendance and spot checks), and it was reported by most practitioners that the use of such measures strengthened anti-oppressive practice through collaborative working with the service users.

Single-case designs used

Altogether, a total of 125 designs were used in the 83 cases (Table 3.2). The designs that include letters A, B and so on represent single-case designs, whereas the pretest post-test and qualitative descriptive are not included in the wide range of single-case designs available, as they do not fulfil the requirement of repeated measurement. Therefore, the evaluative inferences (if any) that can be drawn with these designs are weaker than with the B design. The 5 PTD designs refer to the periodic treatment elements design (Barlow, Hayes and Nelsen 1984) which compares changes immediately following treatment sessions. It should be noted that, although one design only was used in 53 cases, more than one design was used in another 29 cases.

Table 3.2   **Numbers and types of single-case research designs used by agency staff**

Type of Design Used	N
B	47
A-B	26
Pretest post-test	12
A (successive interventions)	7
A-B-A	6
Periodic treatment elements design (PTD)	5
A-B + follow-up	5
B (successive interventions)	5
A-B-A-BC	4
Qualitative/descriptive	4
A-B-A-B-A	1
A-B-A-C-D-A	1
A-BC-AD-CD	1
Subtotal	125
Assessments only	7
Measures lost	4
Total systematic evaluation efforts	136

Source: *Kazi and Wilson (1996)*

Table 3.2 indicates that the B design was used most frequently (n = 47), followed by the AB design (n = 26). Four of the A-B designs were replicated across clients, i.e., the same intervention was used by the same practitioner with four. Another three A-B designs were replicated across target problems, i.e., the same practitioner used the same intervention to improve three target problems with the same client. Two of the A-successive interventions' designs were also replicated across two target problems with the same client. The four A-B-A-BC designs were replicated across clients, but with four siblings in the same family. These replications occurred naturally in the course of the social workers' practice, and were not determined by the needs of the research study. These replicated designs allow stronger causal inferences to be made in all of these cases.

Interventions used

Intervention is defined at the broadest level as 'what the practitioner does to affect (change) a problem' (Bloom and Fischer, 1982, p. 241) in a formal, planned, and systematic way. Some of the interventions described by practitioners in this sample include intervention programmes which also involve significant others, such as school teachers (e.g. 'encouragement', 'gradual reintegration' in school). In such circumstances, the intervention activities of the practitioner cannot be evaluated separately from those of the significant others.

Table 3.3 indicates that counselling was by far the most frequently used intervention, followed by mobilising parents, encouraging pupils and making a legal warning to parents, in that order. Unfortunately, as the study concentrated more on specifying and operationalising target problems, the importance of a clear description of interventions was not emphasised enough, e.g. it is not clear how 'behaviour modification' is different from 'behaviour management', or whether 'mobilising parent' was included under 'counselling' by other practitioners.

Table 3.3   The 13 most frequent interventions applied in the sample

Interventions	Number Used
Counselling	47
Mobilising Parent	14
Encouragement	10
Legal Warning	9
Behaviour Modification	7
Building Home-School Links	7
Escorting to School	5
Mobilising Peer Support	5
Lesson Changes	5
Sending Letters Home	4
Gradual Reintegration	4
Behaviour Management	4
Liaison with Medical Staff	4

The 'evaluative' (progress) and 'experimental' (causal) questions

The terms 'evaluative' and 'experimental' are used in a particular sense in the context of single-case designs, as in Thyer 1993. The 'evaluative' question is whether the target problem changed; and the 'experimental' question is whether there was a causal link between the intervention and the changes in the target problem.

The first key question addressed by single-case designs is the 'evaluative' question, i.e., whether or not the target problem that was the object of the intervention actually changed, and if so, to what extent and in which direction. Table 3.4 indicates the extent to which this question was addressed in the 83 cases included in this study. Here the term 'design' includes all the variables to which measures were applied, and therefore all of the 136 designs used (including the 11 in Table 3.2 which were not really research designs as the measures were used for assessment purposes or were lost by the respondents) are considered in Table 3.4.

Table 3.4   The extent to which the designs address the 'evaluative' question

The 'Evaluative' Question	(n = 136)
Some significant improvement at the onset of the intervention.	112
Some deterioration at the onset of the intervention.	3
Target problem does not improve or deteriorate.	9
Data cannot address this question.	12

Of the 136 target problems which were operationalised, the designs used indicate that at the onset of the intervention(s), 112 (or 82%) improved significantly, 3 became worse and there was no change in another 9. The evaluative question could not be addressed in 12 because the measures were used for assessment purposes only (i.e., once only), the measures were used but lost, or the qualitative descriptive indicator used could not enable this question to be addressed. In terms of the cases rather than the numbers of target problems involved, overall there was deterioration in 1 case and the target problem remained unchanged in 3 cases. In 76 cases (or 92%) there was a significant improvement in at least one target problem.

The second key question addressed by single-case designs is the extent to which the intervention was responsible for the change in the target problem, i.e., whether a causal inference can be drawn from the findings, and if so to what extent can such an inference rule out alternative explanations. Table 3.5 illustrates the extent to which this question is addressed in the 83 cases included in this study.

Table 3.5   The extent to which the designs address the 'experimental' question

The 'Experimental' Question	N
The design does not address this question.	80
Causal inference can be drawn but very weak	28
Causal inference can be drawn with some confidence	13
Causal inference can be drawn with a high degree of confidence	15

The extent to which the 'experimental' question is addressed depends on the single-case design used as well as the indications from the trends in the data, e.g. whether or not there is an immediate, sharp improvement at the onset of the intervention, and whether the trend is in the opposite direction when the intervention is withdrawn. Table 3.5 indicates that of the 136 designs used (i.e. 136 target problems that were operationalised), 80 (or 59%) were unable to address this question, but 56 (or 41%) allowed causal inferences to be drawn ranging from weak to a relatively high degree of confidence. This finding is not surprising as the strategy of this study was to concentrate on operationalising target problems and measurement, whilst allowing the design to be determined naturally in the course of practice.

In the event, the largest number of designs used was the B design which addressed the 'evaluative' but not the 'experimental' question. This finding is consistent with that of Mutschler (1984) who also found that instruments aimed at evaluating progress and achievement of treatment outcomes were more likely to be used with a larger number of clients than experimental research designs examining the differential effectiveness of interventions (p.336-7). Despite its limitations, the B design appeared to lend itself to the needs of practice in 47 cases in this study; however, it should be noted that more than one design was used in most of these cases, providing useful information to both social workers and their clients.

Table 3.6   **Total ratings of all the specified reasons for using the study's evaluation strategies in the order of preference**

Reason	Rating
Help with identification of problems and assessment	16
Provide evidence of improvement to the school	17
Make social work practice more effective	18
Provide evidence of improvement to the client	18
Help in more objective reporting in case conferences	18
Evaluate effectiveness of particular interventions	18
Promote a more objective and systematic approach	18
Make the agency more accountable	19
Provide evidence of improvement to the social worker	20
Improve the image of the agency	20

1 = strongly agree, 2 = somewhat agree, 3 = disagree

Source: *Kazi and Wilson (1996)*

Feedback from social workers

Twelve social workers who attended a training session towards the end of the study responded to a post-study questionnaire. Of these, two had not participated in the study, citing lack of time as the main reason. They indicated that they had missed the study's training sessions and also felt that the measures devised by the other participating social workers were not necessarily relevant in their own work. This was in keeping with the views expressed by a minority of social workers in meetings at the start of the study, namely that the pressures of time in their work meant that they were not prepared to take on anything new which added to those pressures. Furthermore, as the agency was having to reduce its workforce, they felt that evaluation was not a priority for them.

The other ten respondents had taken part in the study. When asked to rate the reasons for using the study's evaluation strategies (see Table 3.6), the respondents indicated that they were more concerned with the identification of problems and providing evidence of progress to schools then with the image of the agency and evidence of progress for the practitioners. The other reasons were placed in the middle of this continuum, including making the agency more accountable and social work more effective, providing evidence of improvement to the client, and promoting a more objective and systematic approach.

Table 3.7   **Number of respondents (n = 10) who rated their skills before and after the study on a scale of very skilled, somewhat skilled, and not skilled**

	Very Skilled		Somewhat		Not Skilled	
	Before	After	Before	After	Before	After
Assessment of client problems and needs	5	5	5	5	0	0
Describing problems in measurable terms	2	5	7	5	1	0
Involving client in identifying problems	7	8	2	2	1	0
Involving client in measuring problems	0	2	8	8	2	0
Monitor client change over time (for problems other than school attendance)	2	2	7	8	1	0

Source: *Kazi and Wilson (1996)*

When asked to rate their skills before and after the study on a scale of 'very skilled'. 'somewhat skilled' and 'not skilled' (Table 3.7), five respondents considered themselves 'very skilled' in making assessments of client problems and needs, and the other five rated themselves as 'somewhat skilled', both before and after the study. This finding indicates that the social workers considered themselves to be generally skilful in making assessments, and that the study had no impact in this area. However, there was a marked impact in the involvement of clients in the identification of problems, and some impact on all of the other skills identified in Table 3.7.

Follow-up studies at Kirklees: truancy and disaffection projects

The agency-wide study at Kirklees encouraged practitioners to incorporate single-case evaluation procedures into their daily practice. Following on from this study, similar procedures were used to evaluate specific, government-funded truancy and behaviour projects (Kazi, Craven and Wilson 1995). These projects provided opportunities to continue extensive use of these evaluation procedures alongside general programme evaluation procedures. As previously, the emphasis was on enabling practitioners to evaluate their own practice, and to disseminate their findings to promote good practice. All projects were required to specify their aims and objectives, and indicators of progress. In all cases involving work with specific pupils or groups of pupils, it was agreed that single-case evaluation procedures would be used as applied in the earlier agency-wide study. Two of these evaluations are included in the foregoing---the first, Whitcliffe Mount (also reported in Kazi 1997) is an example of the use of periodic treatment elements designs (PTD--see Chapter 2), as well as illustrating a procedure for aggregating the results from a number of single-case designs to enable judgements regarding the effectiveness of a particular project or programme. The second, Fartown, is an example of a pre-planned use of ABA designs to evaluate a group work programme.

Project Whitcliffe Mount

This school-based project consisted of a teacher and a social worker, working to supplement existing provision at the school by providing a rapid response which was one of the strengths of this on-site project. It was decided to concentrate efforts on year 10 pupils, using the same intervention programme in every case. The overall aim was to identify persistent absentees and re-integrate them into school. This process included investigation of the reasons for non-attendance and implementing programmes of intervention to help deal with those reasons. Pupils and parents were invited to meetings with the project staff in a caring environment, reducing formalities to a minimum. Such meetings took place at the school, home or at other mutually acceptable sites. The staff approached each situation positively, whilst still emphasising the disruptive and destructive consequences of truancy. The staff stressed that they were there to provide as much help as possible to remove the conditions which caused truancy, and to remove the barriers of fear and alienation which prevented the pupil returning to school after a period of truancy.

Specific targets were set for individual pupils, and educational support was provided within the school to help in the re-integration of persistent absentees. For example, pupils who demonstrated progress in attendance received praise from the head teacher. The key indicators of progress used included an examination of attendance record sheets and the creation of personal achievement charts to help monitor and evaluate progress with all concerned.

The project staff worked directly and intensively with fifteen pupils and their parents, constructing personal achievement charts for each pupil and using single-case evaluation to monitor progress. For each of the fifteen cases, the measure used was the school attendance register, expressed as percentage attendance per school week. The baseline consisted of the first few weeks immediately preceding the first contact made with the pupil and/or parent. The changes in the levels of attendance following each contact demonstrate both whether progress was made, and the extent to which such progress could be attributed to the work of the project team i.e., the degree of attributable confidence. The designs used in this project are an application of the 'periodic treatment elements design' as described in Barlow, Hayes and Nelson (1984, p. 210). This design enables the examination of trends in the data following specific contacts (e.g. letters home, meetings with parents) between the project staff and the pupil and/or parents. If a consistent pattern emerges between the periodicity of intervention elements and the periodicity of behaviour change, then inferences can be drawn regarding the effectiveness of the intervention. Therefore, using the principle of successive coincidences, this design can address both the 'evaluative' and 'experimental' questions (Thyer 1993, and as described in Chapter 2). If it can be shown more than once that there were improvements immediately after such contacts, then causal inferences can be drawn with some confidence.

Analysis of individual cases

For each of the fifteen cases, the measure used was the school attendance register, expressed as percentage attendance per school week. The baseline consisted of the first few weeks immediately preceding the first contact made with the pupil and/or parent. The changes in the levels of attendance following each contact demonstrate both whether progress was made, and the extent to which such progress can be attributed to the work of the project team. Table 3.8 aggregates the findings from all 15 cases; and three of these cases (Figures 3.14-3.16) are illustrated here as examples of the extent to which inferences can be drawn from periodic treatment element designs (PTDs) in terms of both the evaluative and experimental questions.

The first case example is that of DK (Figure 3.14). The baseline attendance was a stable zero, but considerable progress was achieved in raising attendance levels to 50%, 100% and 90% in the weeks following the intervention. Figure 3.14 indicates that contacts made were immediately followed by progress on three occasions; hence this progress was most probably attributable to the intervention.

The second example is that of ET (Figure 3.15). The baseline attendance levels were 50%, down to 0% in the week prior to the intervention. Subsequent contacts on two occasions led to immediate improvements, leading to 100% attendance in each of the following seven weeks. Therefore, progress was made, and the two 'coincidences' indicate that the changes were probably attributable to the intervention, although alternative explanations cannot be ruled out. At the end of the 7 week period of 100% attendance, ET failed to attend for two weeks, despite further contacts made by the team. Nevertheless, on the whole, it can be concluded that considerable progress was made in this case.

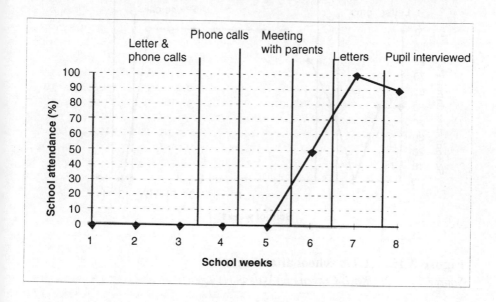

Figure 3.14   DK's school attendance
Source: *Kazi, Craven and Wilson (1995)*

The third example of PW illustrates a PTD design as well as a standard ABC single-case design (Figure 3.16). The baseline phase A indicates attendance of between 30 and 70%. The subsequent contacts made by the project team (intervention Phase B) actually led to a deterioration in attendance. It was not until the meeting was arranged at the local authority's Attendance Panel (Phase C) that considerable progress was made. The Attendance Panel is a meeting between parents and local authority officials where statutory powers can be invoked, e.g. prosecution of parents for failing to ensure their child's regular attendance at school. It can be concluded that progress was made, and that it was slightly attributable to the efforts of intervention B followed by the Panel meeting, intervention C (where contracts were agreed). As there was only one intervention event that was followed by immediate and marked progress, alternative explanations cannot be ruled out. At best, the trend in this chart (Figure 3.16) indicates a slight hint (not most probable or even probable, but slightly probable) that the attendance panel meeting caused the observed improvement in school attendance.

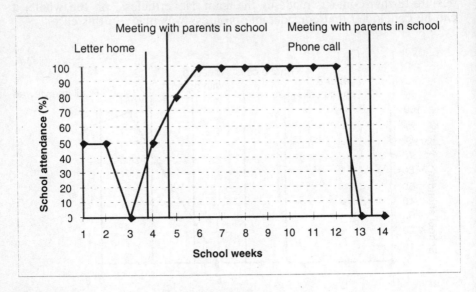

Figure 3.15   ET's school attendance
Source: *Kazi, Craven and Wilson (1995)*

The aggregation of single-case designs in this project is based on indications regarding the extent to which progress was made in each case, and the extent to which this progress could be attributed to the project's intervention. The fifteen cases where the project team were involved in some depth were all successful in achieving higher levels of attendance (see Table 3.8), and therefore the evaluative question was addressed in all cases. In five of these cases, the progress made can be most probably attributed to the team's efforts; in another nine cases the team's efforts were probably responsible; and in only one case the progress made is slightly attributable to the team's intervention. These fifteen designs could be considered to be quasi-multiple baseline designs---quasi because the interventions are not applied to each case sequentially, hence not following a basic requirement (Bloom, Fischer and Orme 1995). Nevertheless, on the whole, there is overwhelming evidence that this project was effective in its work, and that the intervention programmes were successful in helping pupils achieve higher levels of attendance across all 15 cases.

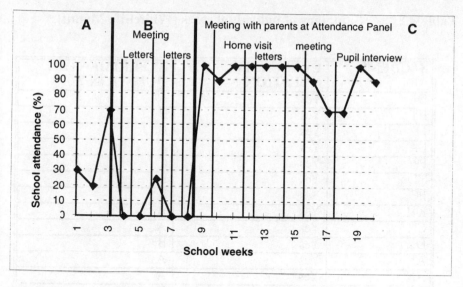

Figure 3.16 **PW's school attendance**
Source: *Kazi, Craven and Wilson (1995)*

All of these cases followed the strategy that single-case designs could themselves unfold along with practice, and be made flexible to fit the needs of practice. The designs used in this project are particularly useful where the intervention programme is characterised by particular events, such as meetings with school pupils and their parents, changes in agreements made with clients, specific counselling sessions, and so on. By tabulating the extent to which the evaluative and experimental questions are addressed in each case, it is possible to make a judgement regarding the overall efficacy of a particular project or programme. In the case of Project Whitcliffe Mount, it can be concluded that 1) progress was made in all 15 cases; and 2) that in 14 cases it can be demonstrated in varying degrees that the project's interventions 'were responsible for the improvements in school attendance.

Project Fartown

Project Fartown was based in one secondary school, and consisted of the equivalents of half a teacher and half a social worker. The aims were to raise awareness of the importance of good attendance, the need for parents' authorisation of genuine absences, and to provide incentives for improving school attendance. It was decided to concentrate on year 9 pupils, mainly through group work with pupils nominated by form tutors. The main criteria for inclusion was where the pupils' behaviour

Table 3.8   Summary of individual cases (Whitcliffe Mount)

STUDENT	EVALUATIVE QUESTION ?	EXPERIMENTAL QUESTION ?
DK	Yes	A
ET	Yes	B
JT	Yes	B
LA	Yes	A
PW	Yes	C
TD	Yes	B
PF	Yes	B
KH	Yes	B
CH	Yes	A
DL	Yes	B
AL	Yes	A
AN	Yes	A
AO	Yes	B
CS	Yes	B
MS	Yes	B

Key	
Evaluative Question?	**Experimental Question?**
Whether progress was made: **Yes** **No**	Whether the progress is attributable to the intervention: **A** = Most probably attributable **B** = Probably attributable **C** = Slightly attributable

Source: Kazi, Craven and Wilson (1995)

was such that it impeded their progress or that of the rest of the form groups. In order to help develop personal and social skills, the group work included separate Personal and Social Skills' (PSE) teaching and English lessons taught in small groups. For all other subjects a normal time-table was followed by these pupils. Students were allocated to the group following parental approval. Tokens were awarded for good behaviour, leading to other rewards such as letters of commendation and trips to a centre for motorcycle riding. Community placements were also provided at the local junior school, at the technical college's textile department, and at a day centre for older people.

Additional support was provided by the social worker for the pupils, their siblings and their parents. Approval was sought and gained from all parents for inclusion into the group, following extensive discussions with the social worker. Regular home visits were made to report on progress and to clarify school issues with parents. These visits also helped the school teachers to gain a better understanding of the pupils' home circumstances. Of the 19 chosen for the group, all had problems of behaviour and 13 had problems of attendance. Single-case evaluation was used with the fifteen pupils who continued as regular participants of the group which began in September 1994 and terminated in January 1996. The measures used were the school attendance register and qualitative data of the parents' perceptions obtained from semi-structured interviews with parents at home following the termination of the group work.

Every family involved in the group work project was visited at home following the termination of the intervention. The social worker interviewed the parents, using a semi-structured format and open-ended questions (Robson 1993) to obtain their perception of the impact of the groupwork project Fartown on their children The unanimous response from all parents was that their children had benefited from this intervention. Comments made included:

I could not get him out of bed...now he's up without me shouting.

He couldn't wait to get a 'good boy' letter.

It's been good getting nice letters from school...he always used to be in trouble.

He now has friends and likes school more

He's much more pleasant at home, is more confident and talks positively about school.

Single-case design charts were constructed and shared with each of the 15 participants in the group. The measure used was the percentage of attendance at school per month. The resulting single-case evaluation design was the ABA design, the first phase A being the baseline before the intervention, the second phase B being group work, and the third phase A representing the return to baseline following the end of the intervention. This design fitted in appropriately, as the group work was time-limited from the outset, and in the meantime the school attendance register was taken anyway as a matter of daily school routine.

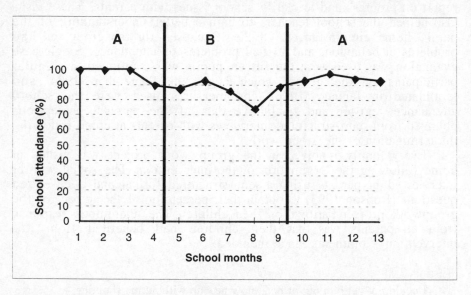

Figure 3.17   CJ's monthly school attendance
Source: *Kazi, Craven and Wilson (1995)*

Figure 3.17 (CJ's chart) is an example of four cases where attendance did not improve but actually deteriorated during the groupwork programme (intervention phase B). Of course, when evaluating practice the practitioner has to be prepared for data confirming that the intervention programme may have contributed to a deterioration rather than an improvement of the target problem. The qualitative feedback from parents indicates that they were satisfied with the project---and yet there is a worsening of the situation in four cases. The project workers explained that another aim of the group was to improve behaviour in school---and that behaviour actually improved in all cases (the indicators of progress used to corroborate this were qualitative perceptions of teachers and parents), although this was not matched by school attendance in these four cases.

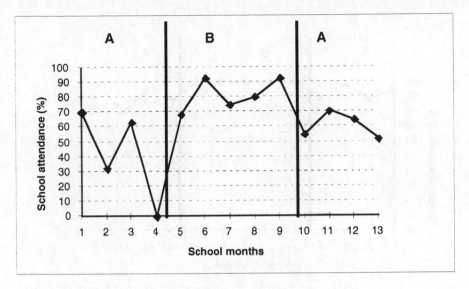

Figure 3.18   **SS's monthly school attendance**
Source: *Kazi, Craven and Wilson (1995)*

Apart from the four cases where attendance worsened, the evaluative question---whether the client's target problem improved or not---was addressed in 11 out of the 15 cases. In the 11 cases where progress was made, attendance immediately dropped somewhat when the group work ceased in 9 cases, indicating through two successive 'coincidences' that the improvement in attendance was probably attributable to the group work. Figures 3.18 and 3.19---charts of SS and TJ respectively---are two examples from these 9 cases, illustrating the classic patterns of ABA designs (see Chapter 2). In all of these 9 cases, the absolute levels of attendance were higher in the follow-up phase A than in the initial baseline phase A, indicating positive carry-over effects of the programme months after it ceased to operate with these pupils. However, a downward trend does provide a second coincidence which helps to provide a stronger causal link between the intervention and its effects.

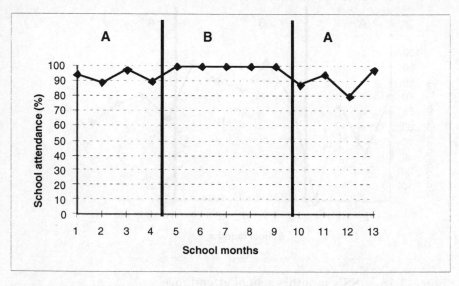

Figure 3.19   TJ's monthly school attendance
Source: *Kazi, Craven and Wilson (1995)*

In another two cases, attendance did not drop immediately after the group work ceased, hence indicating that there may have been alternative explanations for the progress in the B phase, and therefore the progress was only slightly attributable to the group work in these two cases (Figure 3.20---MC's chart---is an illustration of one of these two cases). Of course, from the point of view of clinical significance, the project workers were more than happy to see progress maintained after the groupwork programme ceased---but if there is immediate progress after the intervention started, but no downward trend in the data after it stopped, then the design's ability to make a casual link is no better than the AB design (see Chapter 2) which provides only one indication, or a slight hint, that the improvement was caused by the programme. This was pertinent here also because the groupwork project began in the month of September, when usually attendance is better than towards the end of the school year--therefore attributable confidence was an important element in the evaluation of this programme's effectiveness.

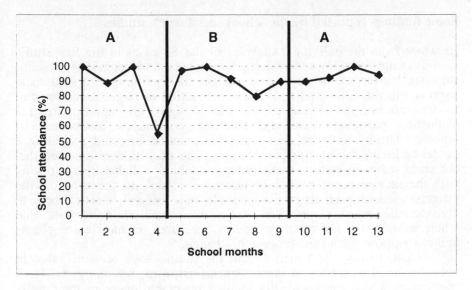

Figure 3.20   MC's monthly school attendance
Source: *Kazi, Craven and Wilson (1995)*

On the whole, therefore, there is evidence from the attendance patterns observed in the single-case evaluation charts that in the majority of cases the group work intervention was effective in improving attendance. When the findings from the fifteen ABA single-case designs are combined with the qualitative data of the parents' perceptions of progress, it can be concluded that the group work was effective in achieving its stated aims. The successes were achieved with pupils with a record of absenteeism and disruption who benefited from the innovative way in which the group work operated. For the purposes of groupwork, the pupils were withdrawn from two subjects; the groupwork consisted of alternative lessons in these two subjects, with a greater emphasis on building positive attitudes amongst the pupils. In this project, the ABA design was used as it fitted the needs of practice, and single-case evaluation was combined with qualitative interviews with the parents of the pupils to obtain their perceptions regarding the impact of groupwork on the pupils. The same intervention was used across 15 clients, and therefore these designs could be considered to be quasi-experimental multiple baseline designs as in the Whitcliffe Mount project---themselves enabling a causal link between the intervention and its effects. Even when taken individually, attributable confidence was indicated by the patterns of the ABA designs in 9 out of the 15 cases---providing evidence that the project was responsible for the observed improvements in the target problem of school attendance in the majority of the cases.

Some findings reported by the school social work studies

Evidence from the individual analyses of the 83 cases in the first study, as well as the cases from the subsequent truancy and behaviour projects, suggests that the use of single-case designs has encouraged a systematic approach in the definition and operationalisation of target problems and in the monitoring of outcomes. The designs are appropriate for evaluating particular casework, enabling continuous assessment of outcome data by both the clients and the practitioners, and providing a model of accountability for practitioners. The practitioners reported that the single-case evaluation methodology enabled collaborative working with the service users, providing regular feedback to the user on the progress made at each stage. For example, in a research meeting held to consider the report of the first study, the practitioners reported that where appropriate self-report measures were used, in most cases clients had felt empowered in the process of change.

In conclusion, the benefits from the studies have been of value to both the social workers and their clients. First, a methodology has been introduced which can be readily applied by practitioners in their daily practice and enable them to become practitioner evaluators. The fact that 21 practitioners applied the single-case evaluation methodology in 83 cases, as well as in the subsequent truancy and behaviour projects, are indications of their enthusiasm to become practitioner evaluators. Second, this methodology can address both the evaluative and experimental questions in varying degrees, depending upon the designs used and the trends in the data. Such information can be of benefit to both social workers and their clients. Third, the effectiveness of practitioners has been demonstrated in a large majority of the cases included in the studies, a high degree of effectiveness which otherwise may have gone unnoticed. Finally, this methodology is now part of the daily repertoire of Kirklees Education Social Work Service's social workers, and will remain with them indefinitely, to be used, refined, and further developed to suit the needs of both the clients and the practitioners in the foreseeable future. The changes in the agency's recording practices to facilitate the application of single-case evaluation technology is an indication of the long-term benefits of these studies.

The few studies that have been published to date on the application of single-case evaluation technology have highlighted, amongst other things, the need for organisational support systems, the demonstration of the technology's utility and benefits, appropriate training for social worker practitioners and their involvement in the further development of this methodology (Robinson, Bronson and Blythe 1988; Mutschler 1984). These recommendations were implemented in Kirklees studies with positive results. These studies indicate, in particular, that success in any effort at agency-wide application of this technology depends upon the support and encouragement of social workers by the agency's management, the dissemination of initial experiences in the application of this methodology throughout the agency, a fairly intensive programme of training and consultancy provision for the practitioners, and the involvement of practitioners in the construction of measuring instruments and the development of the methodology itself in order to maintain its relevance to their practice. The fact that such a high proportion of practitioners applied this methodology corroborates the findings of these other studies, and indicates that these factors should be considered in any other similar study in the future.

The strategy of placing practice considerations as paramount, and research considerations as secondary, was in keeping with the recommendation of Bloom and Fischer (1982). This strategy consisted of concentration on the basic requirements of single-case evaluation rather than the research designs themselves, allowing the designs to be applied flexibly to the needs of practice. Hence, the ethical considerations regarding withdrawal of intervention programmes did not arise, as all withdrawals were made naturally in the course of practice. The main benefits reported by practitioners included the systematic approach and evaluative feedback for both social workers and clients.

The avoidance of complicated statistical tests enabled the practitioners to concentrate on the fundamental principles of single-case evaluation, and to place the emphasis on evaluation. Experimental designs (i.e., those which allow comparisons between the intervention and non-intervention phases in order to establish a causal link between the intervention and its effects, even though such links would be weak and tentative) were used wherever possible, and practitioners were encouraged from the positive results indicated in the vast majority of cases. The practitioners also found that, whilst it was desirable to place the emphasis on using the designs as indicators of client progress rather than on experimental ones, in some cases where the B design was used, a few additional activities--for example, the construction of retrospective baselines for school attendance--may have enabled the experimental (causal) question to be addressed in those cases as well. The proposed changes in the agency's recording systems would encourage the construction of such retrospective baselines wherever possible.

In keeping with Blythe and Rodgers (1993) methodological shifts (i.e. emphasis away from experimental designs), the study demonstrates that the full range of single-case designs are available to the social worker, and not only those that are experimental. For example, in the first study, the B design was used most frequently (47 times), followed by the AB design (26 times). Four of the AB designs were replicated across clients with the same target problem, and another three across target problems with the same client. Withdrawal--or return to baseline conditions--was used in 19 designs, including an ABABC design replicated across four clients with the same target problem. These replicated designs occurred naturally in the course of practice and allowed stronger causal inferences to be made in all of the cases where they were used.

A further consideration worth noting from the Kirklees studies is the use of both qualitative and quantitative measures, in keeping with the modern definition of measurement (Bostwick and Kyte 1993) and texts which suggest such mixing is possible (Brennan 1992). The use of qualitative measures such as the ABC chart (client self-log) enriched the evaluation process for both the social workers and their clients, particularly in the cases where both qualitative and quantitative measures were used. Further, the use of single-case designs supplemented the routine, qualitative process-recording already taking place in the agency.

Another finding is that single-case evaluation techniques are applicable to non-behavioural target problems---even though the majority of the 136 specified problems reported in the first study were those of behaviour (including school absenteeism), there were a significant number involving effects of sexual abuse, family tragedy, self-esteem, and so on. As for intervention programmes, the vast majority of the 136 were non-behavioural (e.g. 47 involved counselling). These findings are of particular significance in view of Robinson, Bronson and Blythe 's (1988) review which found that reports of application of this methodology in non-behavioural situations were rare. Taken together with the use of qualitative measures as indicated earlier, it can be concluded that although single-case evaluation originated from quantitative and behavioural approaches, the methodology is no longer restricted to these approaches, and is developing towards a wider application in social work practice.

4 Examples of Research in a Probation Service

A recent project in a probation service (Kazi and Hayles 1996, Kazi 1998, Hayles and Kazi 98) illustrates the application of another agency-wide approach to enable practitioners to use effectiveness research. The author worked with all 12 students (and their 7 practice teachers) on final placements with West Yorkshire Probation Service in 1996 to encourage them to use single-case evaluation to demonstrate the effectiveness of Probation Orders with adult offenders that they were supervising as part of their practice. This evaluation project was commissioned by the agency and began in response to the internal and external pressures on probation services to be more accountable to society and to demonstrate the effectiveness of their work. According to McGuire and Priestley (1995, p. 24):

> There is a responsibility...for the creation of a culture of empirical evaluation: for an atmosphere in which programme design, delivery and evaluation are seen as natural accompaniments to each other, and for the habit of evaluation to become firmly embedded in the thinking of managers and practitioners alike.

Part of this process is the growing need for students on qualifying courses (i.e., trainee probation officers) to provide evidence of their ability to evaluate the effectiveness of their work (CCETSW 1989). It was felt that the students on final placements would benefit from an evaluation project to enable them to evaluate their practice; and that, at the same time, the experiences generated could provide a catalyst for developing the use of evaluation procedures within the agency as a whole.

Strategy

The strategy used by the evaluator to promote the use of single-case evaluation procedures was a replication of that used in the Kirklees Education Social Work Service (see Chapter 3), adapted to the probation setting, as follows:

1. The starting point was the desire of agency managers to demonstrate the effectiveness of their services. Negotiation with them included the role of the researcher as a salesperson for single-case evaluation in order:
   a) to facilitate the agency's search for a method that could be integrated within the daily practices of the service;
   b) to enable collaboration with service users to monitor progress with each case;
   c) to enable an aggregation of data to demonstrate the effectiveness of the service to external stakeholders.

2. The leading service managers (in this project the senior probation officers who manage training and practice teaching) themselves participated in the effort, frequently reassuring both staff and students that:
   a) the data will be handled in confidence and with sensitivity in the interests of both practitioners and users;
   b) appropriate time will be allocated for the project, particularly at the initial stages, and that support for the project has been obtained from the highest level possible (in this case the Assistant Chief Probation Officer) to help motivate staff.
The reassurances included an account of the benefits to the agency from demonstrating its effectiveness.

3. The agency staff as a whole (in this project, the practice teachers and the students) were introduced to the principles and requirements of single-case evaluation. This included the most recent accounts of the methodology in the professional press (such as in *Research on Social Work Practice*) illustrated with specific examples and with as little academic jargon as possible. The senior probation officers helped to prevent the author from slipping into such jargon during the training and consultation sessions. The senior probation officers played a leading role in these sessions and chaired the proceedings where appropriate.

4. The training included an introduction into the concepts of measurement, reliability and validity, again with practical

examples in a language designed to encourage practitioners themselves to take part in the discussion. The trainee probation officers were introduced to standardised measures of proven reliability (namely those in Fischer and Corcoran 1994), but cultural factors were also taken into account (e.g. American measures in a British social work context).

5. At an early stage, the strategy moved from a basic introduction to asking practitioners to discuss particular cases from their recent or current practice. They were enabled to go from global to specific descriptions of target problems and to determine what outcome measures might be appropriate. In this process of assessment, they were encouraged to work in a collaborative way with the service user. All the trainee probation officers were encouraged to take part in this discussion, using examples they were willing to share with one another and with the authors Kazi and Hayles (1996).

6. The strategy emphasised that practice considerations were paramount, and that evaluative research served practice. The participants were introduced to the range of single-case designs available (see Chapter 2), from exploratory to explanatory, without over-emphasising the more complicated explanatory designs. The process enabled the practitioner to implement the basic requirements of setting goals, specifying target problems, and assigning appropriate measures in the course of practice, allowing the single-case design to fall into place naturally. Where possible--and only where possible--baseline measures were to be taken before intervention, and follow-up measures after intervention.

7. Only those measures which were appropriate for the practice were to be used. From the discussion of cases, an inventory of potential target problems and potential measures was built, and the group began the construction of their own measures. Bloom Fischer and Orme (1995) and Blythe and Tripodi (1989) were used to guide the process, avoiding complicated statistics. The use of computers in this process was encouraged only if they were available and the staff already used them in their routine practice; otherwise a back-up service was offered to help in the charting of data, at least in the initial stages. The group was informed that standardised measures had higher reliability, but this point was not laboured. If they constructed basic client self-report rating scales, the discussion was negative, but positive, e.g., working out how reliability of the scale could be enhanced, and how it could be developed further.

8. Once the single-case designs fell into place in the course of practice (e.g. whether they were B or AB designs as described in Chapter 2), the practitioners were helped to draw appropriate inferences from the data, bearing in mind limitations such as errors in measurement, inappropriateness of the measures selected, and other considerations they may have discussed with the user.

9. Together with the service managers, the author provided on-going consultancy and support, and in addition, arranged several meetings with the whole staff group. As this particular probation service was scattered in teams across a fairly large area of Yorkshire, individual team meetings of trainee probation officers were arranged where both the local practice teachers and the author were present. From the second meeting onwards, the discussion was based on the actual experience of using single-case evaluation even if, by the time of the second meeting, only a few practitioners had used the method. The practitioners who had actually used the method were encouraged to take centre stage and share their experience with others who were still at the planning stage.

10. Recording systems were developed or amended to facilitate the process of evaluation, avoiding duplication of lengthy narratives. The measurement of outcomes became an integral part of the case recording systems, and formats of potential measures were provided and kept readily at hand.

11. Arrangements were made in advance regarding the forwarding of data to the manager and/or the researcher for the purposes of aggregation and inclusion into a research report, which was prepared by the researcher together with the agency (Kazi and Hayles 1996). Once the data had been aggregated and the report prepared, a draft was taken back to the staff group for discussion. The discussion included experiences of single-case evaluation, including its advantages and limitations, and recommendations for developing the process further. A follow-up meeting with the staff group and senior management was arranged in order to present the final report and to assess progress made and the potential for future developments.

Single-case evaluation procedures

Single-case evaluation procedures included the use of recording systems to identify objectives, the intervention programmes and the means of monitoring client progress. The practitioners were encouraged to use published measures of high reliability (standardised measures in Fischer and Corcoran 1994), and also to create their own measures appropriate to the needs of their clients. The practice teachers participated in this process together with the author, to help practitioners create such measuring tools and to help them to select appropriate measures to meet the needs of each particular client. The measures created included a variety of rating scales, client self-report diaries, and other specific measures for monitoring drug and alcohol use, attitudes, and risk factors associated with criminal behaviour.

Single-case evaluation procedures (i.e. repeated measurement) were combined with other classificatory outcome indicators to enable a judgement to be made regarding the extent of progress achieved. These classificatory indicators were:

a) whether tangible changes were made such as obtaining appropriate employment or housing, including steps towards these goals such as joining a job club or approaching housing associations;

b) whether the client was arrested for further offences in the period of supervision;

c) whether the client was breached for failing to comply with the requirements of the probation or licence supervision process.

The purpose of probation supervision is threefold, as defined in the Criminal Justice Act 1991 [section 8(1)]:

- securing the rehabilitation of the offender

- protecting the public from harm from the offender, or

- preventing the offender from committing further offences.

In this context, rehabilitation can be defined as (Roberts 1991, p. 13):

the process whereby offenders acquire the personal and social skills necessary to function as law-abiding citizens, while the values, attitudes and behaviours that they have adopted to support a criminal life style are modified to become more consistent with acceptable social functioning.

For the purposes of aggregating findings from a large number of single-case designs and the classificatory indicators outlined above, Such progress was divided into three categories, as follows:

P+ = 'considerable'--where there is clear evidence of progress in most of the objectives

P = 'progress'--where there is evidence of progress in more than one objective

S = 'some'--where there is evidence of progress in at least one objective.

The outcome was that all twelve trainee probation officers with the agency at the time used single-case evaluation procedures (including 150 outcome measurements) to evaluate the effectiveness of their supervision of Probation Orders with 71 adult offenders. The following are four case examples from this project---the first where considerable progress was achieved in most of the objectives, the second where progress was made in more than one objective, the third where progress was achieved in at least one objective, and the fourth where the situation for the client deteriorated during the period of supervision.

Case example 1: considerable progress

Male offender D was convicted of drink-driving and causing criminal damage and sentenced to 12 months' Probation Order with a condition to attend a local drink-drive programme. He was also disqualified from driving for two years and ordered to pay £105.75 compensation and £75 court costs. In the first supervision session, the trainee probation officer and D agreed the following objectives of the Probation Order (in addition to the requirements of regular supervision and avoiding behaviour likely to lead to further offences) :

1. Explore consequences of alcohol on offending
2. Consider consequences on others
3. Pursue mediation and reparation
4. Take on board issues of bereavement, health, self-esteem, and   personal finances.

The student described the method of intervention during supervision as 'task-centred work within a cognitive/behavioural framework'. The outcome measures selected included an attendance record, a drink diary and a standardised measure for self-esteem.

Attendance

D regularly attended at the drink-drive programme for the specified eight weeks. He also regularly attended supervision sessions at the Probation Office as required.

Drink diary

D regularly completed a drink diary which identified the amount of money he spent daily on alcohol consumption. The data was then charted as the amount spent per week over 11 weeks. Figure 4.1 indicates that the amount spent was very high in the first week; but from then onwards, considerable progress was made in lowering the amount spent to under £10. The reliability of this measure was entirely dependent upon D's honesty; but the trend of improvement was also confirmed by independent reports from staff at the drink-drive programme.

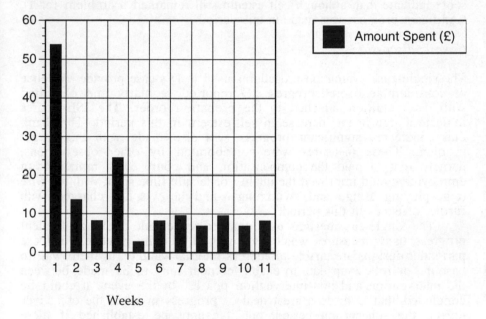

Figure 4.1   Drink diary: amount spent on alcohol consumption per week

Standardised measures from Fischer and Corcoran (1994)

The measure used was Hudson's Index of Self-Esteem (ISE), a 25-item scale designed to measure the 'degree, severity or magnitude of a problem the client has with self-esteem' (Fischer and Corcoran 1994, p. 283). Its reported reliability is high, and it has two cutting scores: scores below 30 (+or-5) indicate absence of a clinically significant problem, and scores above 70 'nearly always indicate that clients are experiencing severe stress with a clear possibility that some type of violence could be considered or used to deal with problems' (ibid., p. 283). The ISE was administered on three occasions, as follows:

Date	Score
3/2/96	131
13/2/96	73
2/4/96	58

The first score indicated a severe problem of self-esteem, which considerably improved at each subsequent occasion. The differences in score indicate that, although self-esteem still remained a problem for D, significant progress was made in this period.

Case 1: discussion

The single-case evaluation procedures used in D's case provide evidence of considerable overall progress. D reported regularly and complied with the condition attached to the probation order. The ISE scores indicate a significant increase in self-esteem in this period. The drink diary indicates significant progress was also made with this target problem. These measures were corroborated by other observations, namely that D paid the compensation and court costs, remained in employment, and improved the quality of leisure time spent with his wife (e.g. playing Bingo and swimming)---and he was not charged with further offences in this period.

   The single-case designs used enabled systematic tracking of client progress, using measures which became part of daily practice, but these particular designs are unable to address internal validity, as there was no baseline or follow-up data to enable comparisons to be made between the intervention and non-intervention phases. In the event, it could be concluded that D made a great deal of progress in all of the objectives during the supervision period, but it cannot be established if these improvements were caused by the Probation Order, or were the result of other factors in the client's circumstances. It could be argued that the above data does not demonstrate the impact of the client's feelings and the effect of his environment, but the Probation Service's recording system required some assessments of these other factors, and although the single-case designs in themselves could not address these questions, they supplemented the essentially qualitative agency records with some objective data reflecting D's achievements.

Case example 2: progress

Male offender G was convicted of shoplifting and resisting arrest, and sentenced to a 12 month Probation Order with a condition to attend an alcohol education group. The trainee supervisor and G agreed the following specific objectives:

1. Encourage reduction in alcohol consumption
2. To support application for custody of his daughter
3. To assist efforts to get rehoused.

The student described the intervention as the use of exercises from a Probation manual 'Targets for Change' (Marshall, Weaver and Loewenstein 1991), as well as liaison with the alcohol education group specified in the Probation Order.

The outcome measures selected included an alcohol drink diary (Figure 4.2) and a record of attendance at supervision sessions (Figure 4.3).

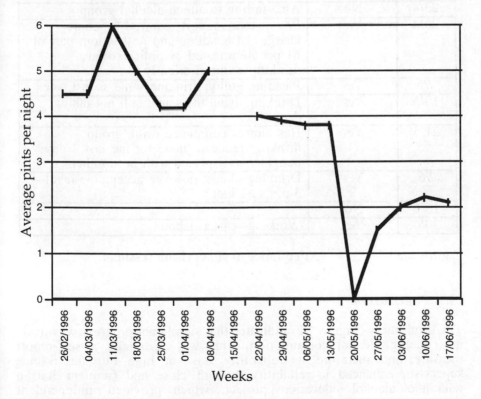

Figure 4.2   Average alcohol consumption per week

Date	Attendance	Notes
20/2	Yes	
28/2	Yes	Completed diary and worksheets; drinks 4.5 pints of cider (about 10 normal strength) per night.
5/3	Yes	Diary not completed; says drinks less when daughter is with him
13/3	Yes	Diary completed; increase in drink
19/3	No	
25/3	Yes	In court for non-payment of fines
2/4	Yes	Daughter truanting; G drinks more
12/4	No	
18/4	No	Home visit--not in
23/4	No	Also failing to attend alcohol group
25/4	Yes	Pre-sentence report required by court--charges of handling and possession; part of 61 people arrested by police so far; drinking reduced slightly
7/5	Yes	Pleading guilty; drinking same as last week
13/5	Yes	Drinking again the same; still not taking drugs
21/5	Yes	Has almost completed drink group; drinking reduced--none for the last 2 days; daughter now placed with her mother
?/6	Yes	Drinking almost down to acceptable level---3 pints a night
13/6	No	
20/6	Yes	Working--casual labour

Figure 4.3   **Attendance at supervision sessions**

Case 2: discussion

The drink diary (Figure 4.2) indicates that significant progress was made in reducing alcohol consumption. This was essentially a self-report measure, and therefore its reliability was not high--but the trainee supervisor enhanced its reliability through close and frequent liaison with the alcohol education project, which provided independent corroboration of the progress made in reducing the levels of alcohol consumption. Apart from this objective, there is also some evidence of progress towards the other objectives. G's success in getting a job (Figure 4.3) was essential for achieving better living conditions and his daughter's custody. However, his arrest for further offences ratifies that, although progress was made, it was not as considerable as in case example 1.

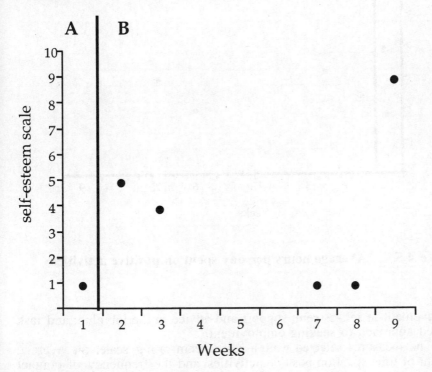

Figure 4.4   Self-esteem ratings (1 = very low to 10 = very high)

Case example 3: some progress

Female adult offender J was convicted of obtaining property by deception and sentenced to a two-year Probation Order. The specific objectives were agreed as follows:

1. Increase self-esteem
2. Improve future employment prospects
3. Maximise income and deal with creditors

The methods of intervention were described by the student as: solution focused interviewing; weekly tasks identified to achieve

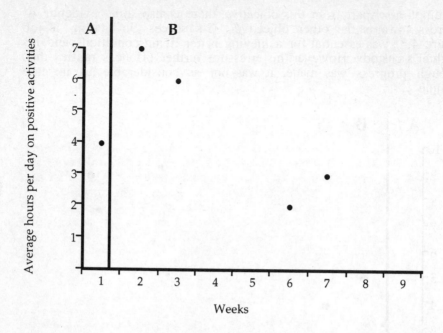

Figure 4.5   Average hours per day spent on positive activities

improvement in self-esteem; support and advice in the job club; and task centred approach to seeking employment.

The measures selected were a self-esteem rating scale, the average amount of time spent on positive activities, and the frequency of contact to meet the reporting requirements of the Probation Order. The self-esteem rating scale ranged from 1= very low to 10 = very high, posing the question 'how do you feel about yourself?', with the results as indicated in Figure 4.4. As this was a retrospective self-report measure regarding the preceding week, the first week could be considered to be a baseline, and therefore the design is AB, indicating a sharp improvement at the onset of the intervention phase B.

The second measure was also a self-report measure, the client recording the average number of hours per day spent on activities 'which make you feel better', worked out as the total number of hours in each week divided by 7 to obtain the average number of hours per day in a given week. Again, as this referred to the preceding week, the first week is taken to be the baseline, and hence Figure 4.5 represents an AB design.

The third measure was the record of attendance at supervision sessions, and it was reported that J attended almost regularly. However, towards the end of the period of study, emotional and financial difficulties led to J not reporting on four consecutive occasions, and she began to cooperate again only after warning of breach proceedings.

Case 3: discussion

J did not offend in the first three months of supervision, but attended the job club on only two occasions and made no progress on her finances. However, she made progress in raising her self-esteem (Figure 4.4) until her ex-partner's return; and then made progress again. Progress was also made in time spent on positive activities (Figure 4.5) when compared to the baseline phase A, although this progress was not maintained. In terms of the specified objectives, progress was made only against one objective, namely self-esteem; and therefore only some progress was made during the period of supervision under study.

Case example 4: deterioration during supervision

This female client was convicted of two counts of common assault and sentenced to a two year Probation Order, with £40 costs and £150 compensation.
The student probation officer agreed the following objectives with the client:

1   To make amends with son's teacher (who was the victim of the assaults)
2   Explore ways of controlling anger
3   To mobilise resources and support
4   To develop coping skills including sleeping at night.

Week	No. of nights T did not sleep	No. of nights of disturbed sleep	No. of nights T slept well
1	4	3	
2	3	3	1
3	5	1	1
4	6	1	
5	2	2	3
6	4	3	
7	1	3	2
8	4	2	

Figure 4.6   **The daily sleep diary**

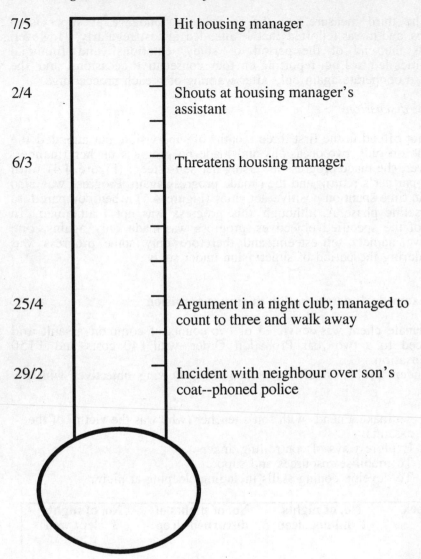

7/5   Hit housing manager

2/4   Shouts at housing manager's
                        assistant

6/3   Threatens housing manager

25/4   Argument in a night club; managed to
                        count to three and walk away

29/2   Incident with neighbour over son's
                        coat--phoned police

Figure 4.7   **The anger thermometer**
Source: *Joanne Trevitt in Kazi and Hayles (1996)*

A composite intervention programme was agreed, with several elements. First, it was agreed that social work services of a voluntary agency---the local Family Service Unit---would be mobilised to help the client in parenting her son. Second, the trainee probation officer agreed to mediate between the school and the client to improve relations in the

Date	Attendance	Notes
30/1	Yes	Home visit--3 children; 1 disabled
6/2	Yes	Carer for parents and grandmother
13/2	Yes	Liaison with family service unit
21/2	No	Child ill
22/2	Yes	Home visit; daughter anorexic
27/2	No	Father ill
29/2	Yes	Home visit; infested with mice
5/3	Yes	
12/3	Yes	
21/3	Yes	Home visit; social worker suggests residential care for father who says no
26/3	No	
2/4	Yes	Home visit; burgled--money stolen; T controls anger at Social Security office
16/4	Yes	
30/4	Yes	
1/5	Yes	
8/5	Yes	Home visit; T had hit housing manager---common assault charge.
9/5	Yes	
14/5	Yes	
22/5	Yes	Home visit; met with school
30/5	Yes	
6/6	Yes	Home visit
11/6		In court; Combination Order and fines and costs to add to previous.
12/6	Yes	Home visit; 'purse stolen'; financing drug misuse herself.
25/6	Yes	

Figure 4.8   The attendance record sheet

interest of both her son's education and the client's own rehabilitation, as the offences took place against a school teacher. Third, it was agreed that the content of the supervision sessions would include counselling to talk through the client's problems (e.g. sleeping at night) and identify those that needed to be worked on. Fourth, the client agreed to attend adult literacy classes as part of her own self-development.

The outcome measures to be used as indicators of progress were identified as a sleep diary, an anger thermometer (a rating scale measuring anger), and the frequency of contact as required by the Probation Order.

A Sleep diary was kept by the client and completed each day, indicating the quality of sleep at night, along three categories: did not sleep, disturbed sleep and slept well (Figure 4.6).

The anger thermometer was a 10-point rating scale, completed by the client whenever an incident took place that made the client angry. This was a self-report measure---the points were selected by the client herself, and the descriptions of the incident were entered at the next supervision session (Figure 4.7).

The third measure was the Frequency of contact of supervision, with brief notes alongside each contact (Figure 4.8). This measure indicated whether the client reported at the probation office, or was at home during a planned home visit or court event, as agreed.

Case 2: discussion

The anger thermometer indicates that although some progress was made at first, the situation worsened at the end. Although the client's frequency of contact was generally satisfactory (the client missed three appointments, but kept the majority), there is no evidence of progress against any of the agreed target problems. There is also no overall progress indicated by the sleep diary. On the whole, it can be concluded that T's situation generally worsened during supervision, and in fact further offences were committed in this period.

Reported findings from the Probation study

In the 71 cases where the single-case evaluation procedures were used, it was found that 26 were drug or alcohol related, in that the offenders were involved in drug or alcohol abuse. At least one measure was used in all cases, but in 27 the only measure used was in relation to the reporting requirement attached to the probation orders, i.e., meeting regularly with the probation officer. Taken together, 150 measures were used in the 71 cases, including 8 drink diaries and 8 drug diaries, and a variety of other self-report diaries and rating scales. Standardised measures from Fischer and Corcoran (1994) were used in 5 cases, and client opinion surveys were used to supplement other measures in 6 cases. A large proportion of the 150 measures were self-report measures, but in many cases the findings were corroborated from the supervising probation officer's own observations, as well as observations from other workers involved in motoring or drug/alcohol projects that some of the offenders were also required to attend.

A particular contribution of this study was an illustration of the variety of ways in which alcohol and drug use can be measured. Consumption was monitored as units consumed per week, average daily consumption in units for each week, the amount of money spent, and the number of days per week when the substance was not consumed.

The 150 outcome measures were used to indicate whether or not progress was made during the period of supervision under study. Such progress was divided into three categories, as follows:

Considerable progress	9
Progress	18
Some progress	19
	46

Number of cases where at least some progress was made	46
No progress	9
Deterioration	16
	n = 71

The findings from single-case evaluation were combined with other outcome data. It was also found that 1) 18 offenders were arrested for further offences during the supervision period, which meant that the majority (53) were not arrested for further offences in the supervision period: and out of the 71, only 10 were subject of breach proceedings for non-compliance with supervision requirements. Therefore, the evidence from all the main outcome indicators used pointed towards positive outcomes for the majority of the 71 clients who were subject of probation orders in the period of the study.

An attempt was made to correlate client outcomes with the social work intervention used. The social work interventions used by the trainee probation officers were variously described; and more than one type was used in 36 cases. The five most frequently reported interventions were related to the outcomes; and the findings were as indicated in Figure 4.9.

The findings indicate that, in terms of client progress as indicated by the outcome measures applied in the sample, 81% of cases where task centred approaches were used led to some progress, as compared with 'targets for change' (also 81%), cognitive/behavioural (77%), solution focused (65%), and counselling (40%). When correlated with arrests for further offences, the percentage of offenders by intervention approach who were arrested, were counselling (40%), solution focused (35%), 'targets for change' (12%), task centred (10%), and cognitive/behavioural (8%).

Method	Cases	Progress	No change	Deterioration	Arrested	Breached
Task centred	21	17	2	2	2	2
Solution focused	17	11	1	5	6	1
'Targets for Change'	16	13	2	1	2	0
Cognitive/behavioural	13	10	3	0	1	1
Counselling	10	4	2	4	4	1

Figure 4.9   Case outcomes by intervention method

However, there were some serious limitations in the way the intervention programmes were categorised by the practitioners. First, The descriptions of the interventions used tended to be implicit rather than explicit, and in most cases where the practitioners used more than one type of intervention, it was not clear what the boundaries were in the applications of definitions such as 'solution focused' and 'task centred'. It was also not clear what was meant by 'counselling'. The 'targets for change' exercises refer to awareness-raising and other exercises in Marshall, Weaver and Loewenstein (1991), which the trainee probation officers tended to regard as constituting a method of social work intervention. This lack of clarity regarding methods of intervention may be due to the fact that probation 'cannot be measured independently of the unique way it is conducted and experienced in a given moment' (Harris 1996, p. 130). Each practitioner brings his/her own personal, aesthetic qualities and skills into the intervention process, and therefore it may not be possible to replicate a given method of intervention in its entirety--at best, a close approximation can be attempted. Even if such an approximation were close enough, the outcome of replication would be difficult to determine because of the unique circumstances and personal characteristics of each offender. What works in one case may not work in another.

In a study of probation cases, Macdonald (1994) found marked differences between probation officers in their use of methods of intervention in the supervision of offenders. These findings are also corroborated in this study. It was found that each of the students had his/her own preferences in the use of intervention programmes, and that each student tended to apply the same programme in all of his/her cases, with some variations. For example, the same practitioner was involved in the first seven cases in the study, and the programme for all seven cases was described as 'cognitive/behavioural and task centred'.

A second limitation was that the single-case designs used were such that there were no baselines in most cases and therefore comparisons could not be made between the intervention and non-intervention phases. Although the designs used could indicate whether progress was made or not in the client target problems, in most cases no causal link could be made between the intervention programmes and such progress. Therefore, any correlations between a particular method of intervention and its effects can only be indicative, and should be the subject of further study---for example, randomised controlled trials that can establish causal links with much greater confidence than single-case designs.

Response of Practitioners

At the end of the project, a meeting was held of all practice teachers and students who participated in this evaluation study. However, some of the students had already completed their placement, and others were nearing completion, and therefore not all of the students or practice teachers attended. Separate questionnaires for practice teachers and students were distributed at this event. Six students and five practice teachers completed and returned the questionnaire.

All six students reported that the project had been at least marginally helpful (and four said it was helpful or very helpful) in assessment, identification of evidence, collaborative monitoring and identifying outcomes with the client. Five of the respondents felt that the project had been at least marginally helpful (three saying it was helpful) in devising measurement tools. However, the usefulness of standardised measures in Fischer and Corcoran (1994) received a mixed response: three said they had been marginally useful, one said they were not useful and another two reported that they had not used the book at all.

Out of the six students, five rated the impact of single-case evaluation on their practice as positive, four said they would use the methodology at least frequently in their future practice, all six felt that these evaluation procedures should be incorporated into probation officers' routine practice in at least some cases, and all six said they would recommend single-case evaluation to colleagues at least sometimes.

Most practice teacher respondents rated the methodology as very helpful (and the rest helpful) in assessment and identification of evidence; and all five said it was at least helpful in collaborative monitoring and in identifying outcomes with clients. However, in the process of devising measurement tools, most rated the project as marginally helpful. The usefulness of Fischer and Corcoran (1994) was rated as marginally helpful by three respondents, with one saying it was helpful and another one rating the book as not at all helpful. All five practice teachers reported that they would use single-case evaluation very frequently in their teaching practice. Four said the methodology had at least a positive impact on their supervision of student practice, and that it should be attempted by probation officers in all cases (one said in some), and all five said they would recommend single-case evaluation to their colleagues.

Some conclusions from the Probation study

The aims of this study were successfully realised in that single-case evaluation procedures were integrated in the day to day, one-to-one interaction between the practitioner and the client---procedures which could enable systematic tracking of client progress during the supervision periods. All twelve students on placement used these evaluation procedures, using 150 measures in 71 cases. It was found that at least some progress was made in 46 cases. Without studies of this type which reflect the effectiveness of what is routine, day-to-day practice in probation services, such effectiveness would probably go unnoticed.

The use of single-case evaluation procedures together with two classificatory outcome indicators (whether the client was arrested for further offences and/or breached for non-compliance) provided additional evidence, enabling a judgement to be made regarding the overall progress of each case. Using these other classificatory outcome indicators, it was found that 53 clients were not arrested for further offences during supervision, and only 10 out of the 71 were subject to breach proceedings for non-compliance with supervision requirements. It can be concluded, therefore, that the intervention programmes used by the students on their final placements with West Yorkshire Probation Service in 1996 were effective in the majority of cases, although there was a significant minority where there was no progress or even a deterioration in the client's circumstances during the period of supervision.

The limitations of the study included a lack of clarity regarding the nature of the intervention programmes, and inadequate categorisation of the exact social work method used. The descriptions of these programmes using terms such as 'cognitive/behavioural' and 'task centred' were not substantiated in the notes of practitioner-client interaction in the majority of cases. Practitioners need to be clear about the requirements in application of the methods of intervention they are using, and to ensure that their practice actually reflects the selected method.

A further possible limitation of this study is that the practitioners who actually used single-case evaluation procedures were students on placement and not qualified probation officers. In all cases, the students were required to take part in the project as a condition of their practice placements. The involuntary nature of their participation may have had a negative impact on their commitment to evaluation; on the other hand, the desire to demonstrate competence may have had a motivating effect. The fact that more than one measure (i.e., more than the minimum of reporting) was used in over half of the 71 cases indicates some degree of a positive commitment to at least attempt the use of single-case evaluation procedures.

A particular contribution of this study is to demonstrate that single-case evaluation can be used to demonstrate the effectiveness of one-to-one supervision between the probation officer and the client. It is a methodology which can be incorporated into the daily probation practice to systematically track client progress, providing useful feedback to both parties. When combined with classificatory outcome indicators of further offending or breach proceedings, single-case evaluation procedures can be used to provide further evidence of the effectiveness of supervision. This study has used single-case procedures to examine the progress made in each case, and then aggregated the results from each to arrive at an inference regarding overall effectiveness of the supervision procedures used in all 71 cases. In this way, single-case evaluation can be used by the practitioners themselves to systematically track progress in each case and then aggregate the results, enabling inferences to be made regarding the overall effectiveness of an entire Probation Service.

5 Examples from Adult Rehabilitation

Unlike the studies in the previous chapters where single-case evaluation was the only---or the main---methodology used within an empirical practice perspective, this chapter provides an exemplar of a methodological-pluralist and pragmatic perspective to evaluation with single-case evaluation playing an important role. Within this perspective, the starting point is the evaluation question(s), and appropriate methods are selected from the full range available to address the effectiveness question(s) negotiated with the stakeholders. This pragmatic approach was used in a multi-method evaluation of a social care project in England---Oakes Villa Rehabilitation Unit in Huddersfield---aimed at helping older people to regain their independence. The effectiveness questions addressed were both formative and summative:

- Was the programme targeted appropriately?
- What was the process of rehabilitation?
- Did the project have the desired impact on the service users?

The evaluation methods applied included secondary analysis, focus group meetings with staff, single-case evaluation and surveys of both service users and social workers (and/or health workers) who had referred them to the unit, to address these effectiveness questions. It was found that this pragmatic, multi-method approach provided a more complete account of effectiveness of the project than that which could have been achieved by any single method or approach. For example, the reductionism of single-case evaluation was compensated by gaining a greater insight into the perceptions of all of the parties involved in the social care project. The richness of the data obtained through the use of both qualitative and quantitative approaches enabled the evaluator to draw more informed inferences regarding the project's effectiveness.

The provision of services to people aged 65 years and over in the health setting has seen many changes in the last few years with the implementation of the 1990 National Health Service and Community

Care Act. The stated purposes of these changes include empowerment of service users to make informed choices, to enable people to be cared for in their own homes where appropriate, and to provide a seamless service where both social services and health authorities are involved (Audit Commission 1992). The Oakes Villa Rehabilitation Unit is one of the initiatives providing intensive services to people who are recovering from an acute condition or are affected by other circumstances which have reduced their capacity to live independently within their own homes.

This rehabilitation unit began its direct work with clients from the first admissions in 1995. It was established with the overall aim of offering a bridge between hospital placement and independent living through the provision of intensive support. This support included social and therapeutic training to re-learn skills and to re-establish self-confidence. The unit offered specialist therapy to improve people's level of independence through the development of both mental and physical daily living abilities.

Quarterly reports of the Rehabilitation Unit's work were prepared regularly, providing detailed data on each client admitted to the unit. The final report (Kazi 1997 and 1998, Kazi and Firth 1997) was based on the data from the period June 1995-March 1997 inclusive, including an analysis of the data on individual clients contained in the quarterly reports (see Table 5.1), the perceptions of the Unit's staff group obtained from focus group meetings, a survey of referring professionals, and a survey of service users. The main purpose of the evaluation was to analyse the evidence available from a variety of sources as a consequence of the methodological-pluralist approach, and to draw inferences on the effectiveness of Oakes Villa Rehabilitation Unit.

The process of rehabilitation

Over the two-year period, the author held several focus group meetings with the unit's staff. The purposes of these meetings were basically two-fold: 1) to analyse the content of the rehabilitation process from the staff's perception; and 2) to build in effectiveness research methods which the staff could use themselves in the course of their practice. The results from (2) are described in the foregoing later on; as for (1), that is the purpose of this section. The process of rehabilitation was analysed repeatedly with the staff through a dialogic process of successive meetings where the process at each stage was analysed in greater depth. The interviews with staff were conducted through twelve focus group meetings over a two-year period, largely as described in Shaw (1996). The purpose was to obtain the staff's perception of the process and value-base of adult rehabilitation---information, understanding and explanation were obtained through a collective group focus on these issues, the group interaction between the workers and the evaluator itself being central to the method of participatory evaluation of the rehabilitation process. Following the meetings, the rehabilitation process and its underpinnings were written up, and bearing in mind that written words may not include tacit understandings, the writing was done together with the staff to ensure that their perceptions were accurately reflected. Through the naturalist focus group interviews, it was found that Oakes Villa's overall aim was to help people achieve a good quality of life, harnessing their own expectations and abilities.

The emphasis is not on their disabilities, but on what they can do positively. They are helped to make informed decisions on what they want to do---whether they want to return home, or live in care. Relatives are also helped to come to terms with the changing realities. Oakes Villa is more like a home than a hospital; it provides the users the space to make important decisions about their future, and the staff aim to provide honest answers and help the users remain in charge of their own destiny. The user is involved in the decision-making process, from admission through to the review system. All relevant records are shared with the users. The user is not given a quick visit to his/her home, but helped to assess the home situation, and to come to terms with any disability in the context of the home situation where he/she may want to return. A decision to go into residential care is not seen as a failure, as the process raises their awareness of what they want to do, what they can do, and what resources are available---thereby enabling an informed choice. For example, one client went into residential care from here after two home visits which enabled her to realise that she was unable to manage at her own home. A rehabilitation assessment at Oakes Villa can be more cost effective in helping users to consider the realistic alternatives, and helping them to achieve their goals. They are able to make informed decisions in more realistic settings, including visits to their own homes to test their abilities. The main decision in the rehabilitation process is that of the client himself or herself---if there is no motivation, then rehabilitation is not possible.

The process of rehabilitation begins from day one at Oakes Villa. The clients are assessed on their abilities in relation to the activities of daily living. Their own wishes are an important part of the assessment, which also takes into account the abilities they had prior to the acute condition. However, perceptions are sometimes not objective. During the admission process, goals are set, and the assessment is conducted in a relaxed, informal way. A care plan is drawn up, and all members of staff work to the same plan, and have the same expectations. This consistency is maintained through daily recording meetings, based on a full assessment of the client over the previous 24 hours. The Activities of Daily Living scale (devised by the staff themselves in consultation with the author---described later) scores are assigned daily, and kept in the client's file. The care plan is updated in relation to the client's abilities, depending on the progress achieved. The care plan covers all the relevant activities of daily living, and the client is informed of progress daily. In this way, they know what to do next to build on the progress achieved on a daily basis.

The staff's intervention plan is specific for each client, and recorded along with the progress. Review meetings are held usually two weeks from admission, involving the client, relatives, social workers and significant others (e.g. hospital staff). The charted progress is reviewed, and detailed plans are formulated for the next stage. All relevant information is shared with the client and other participants in the review meetings. Resources, (e.g. equipment to help with mobility, and social care arrangements in the community) are mobilised and plans made for discharge as required. As part of the rehabilitation process, several visits are made to the client's home. Usually: 1) the layout and surroundings of the client's home are assessed at the first visit; 2) at the next visit, the client will be encouraged to move around the house; 3) then the next step will be preparing and having snacks and meals in the house; and 4) finally, if the client is ready, overnight stays will be arranged at the client's home. Where possible, community resources (e.g. home care) are also involved in this process, prior to the achievement of full rehabilitation. Sometimes, Oakes Villa staff also provide after-hours intervention in the client's own home, prior to the full discharge; however, such support is limited with the scarcity of resources.

The discharge date is set in advance, to enable preparations to be made. Oakes Villa staff will inform all significant persons (e.g. the general practitioner, social services and the family) and then take the client home upon discharge. A follow-up visit is arranged one week after discharge, and all significant agencies and persons are invited to be present. If the discharge goes according to plan, and the client is settled in the early stages, the final follow-up is held six months later; but if the client is not settled or if the equipment provided appears to be unsuitable, further visits are made to help the rehabilitation process. A member of staff will visit the client to assess if the success of the rehabilitation process was being maintained six months after discharge from Oakes Villa.

Oakes Villa's rehabilitation programme is based on a holistic approach to improve the quality of life for the client. Here, the clients are treated as equals, and their wishes are respected and made central to the rehabilitation process. They come here out of choice, they are in control, and the Oakes Villa staff work with them to achieve their own aims. Therefore, 'success' is defined from the client's perspective. If the client's motivation is to return to independent living in his/her own home, and if Oakes Villa is able to facilitate the achievement of this outcome, then that is 'success'. If the client is unsure, and in the course of the rehabilitation process, he/she makes an informed decision to live in residential care, then to help the client achieve this realisation, is also a 'success'. If the client returns to hospital, it is usually expected, because of the clients' medical condition.

'Success' is also the progress they make whilst at Oakes Villa, to regain their dignity and self-confidence, regardless of their final destination.   The staff are committed to this rehabilitation ethos--- providing time and space for the client, and setting realistic goals with them. Sometimes, their families feel that residential care is the only alternative; but once they observe the progress made at this unit, independent living is once again seen as a realistic option. The staff are open and honest with the users regarding the assessment of their abilities, and ensure that they are also fully aware of the risks involved in independent living.

Targeting: needs analysis and admissions

A secondary analysis of records prior to the initiation of the unit found that out of 100 community care assessments made before the unit's services became an option for care planning, 32 of the clients met the admission criteria that was set for the unit. Therefore, this investigation indicated that the unit was being targeted appropriately, with a potential target population of about a third of the clients who are subject of a community care assessment.

Table 5.1 indicates that there were 108 admissions (including 2 re-admissions) to the Unit in the period June 1995 to March 1997 (inclusive), from various sources, but the majority (73, or 68%) were from hospitals. Unfortunately, the author was unable to obtain data for the total number of clients who were subject of a community care assessment in the same period, and therefore it was not possible to ascertain the actual proportion of such clients admitted to the Oakes Villa unit. According to the unit's staff, in the earlier stages of the programme, some inappropriate referrals were picked up in responses to emergency situations. It was estimated that, out of the 108 admissions, about 12 were inappropriate admissions. The staff learnt lessons from this. For example, they now ask more questions, and try to make a more thorough assessment at admission, to ensure that the client is referred because he/she wants to be rehabilitated, and not because the social worker wants him/her to stay in a safe environment without any prospect of rehabilitation (a service which could be provided in a residential home).

A further indication of the extent to which the unit was used is provided by the data in the quarterly reports in relation to bed occupancy levels. It appears that the occupancy levels have remained at generally above 50% (with some rooms remaining at 100%) on average in the period of this study.

Single-case evaluation and other outcome indicators

This part of the multi-method evaluation is based entirely on the data in relation to the clients admitted to the unit, including their characteristics at the point of admission, the progress made during their stay at the unit, and their final destinations (see Table 5.1). As indicated in Chapter 2, a fundamental requirement of single-case evaluation is the measurement of the subject's target problem (i.e. the object of the intervention or treatment) repeatedly over time. The practitioner is required to select an outcome measure that best reflects changes in the subject's condition, and then to apply the same measure over a period of time to enable a systematic tracking of progress. Experimentation, or the establishment of a causal link between the programme and client outcomes, was not an aim of this particular application.

The outcome measure used at the Oakes Villa unit is the Activities of Daily Living Scale, a measure created by the staff themselves in consultation with the author. It is essentially a rating scale ranging from 1 to 7 as follows:

7--independent
6--independent with equipment
5--independent with supervision
4--receiving enabling assistance, i.e., setting the scene
3--receiving slight assistance, i.e. finishing off with partial help
2--receiving moderate assistance. i.e. quite a bit of help to do the task
1--totally dependant, i.e. requiring someone else to undertake the task

The project's staff enhanced the scale's reliability by providing specific examples for anchoring each point on the scale, by agreeing the definitions as precisely as possible within the group as a whole, and by measuring on the scale as a group activity. Each variable (i.e. specified client activity) is assessed daily against the scale, and then expressed as a weekly percentage:

$$\% = \frac{\text{Total of actual scores in the week}}{\text{Maximum possible in the week}} \times 100$$

In some cases, this scale has been used in conjunction with another five-point scale to measure each client's feelings at one point in time in the latter part of each day, indicated by the number of beans the client places in a pot (0=terrible, to 5=excellent). These measures were also combined with a follow-up assessment after discharge from the unit, providing an indication of success in achieving longer-term rehabilitation.

The quarterly reports included single-case evaluation (ADL) charts and/or other assessment data, on each of the clients that received the rehabilitation unit's services. The findings from all the 106 cases evaluated in the period of the study are presented in Table 5.1. This is another example of the aggregation of results from a large number of single-case designs which help to provide an evidence-based judgement regarding a programme's effectiveness. Table 5.1 provides a summary of the main outcome indicators used in this study---where the clients came from to the unit, the progress made during their stay at the unit (based on the ADL single-case designs charts), their destinations upon discharge from the unit, and where they were at the point of follow-up assessment. Table 5.1 also provides supplementary information regarding the clients' gender, age and medical condition that led to the initial loss of independence. The following are three examples from the 106 clients whose progress was systematically tracked in the evaluation period. To protect the clients' identities and privacy, each client in the foregoing examples is allocated a number which is consistent with the numbering system in Table 5.1.

Client no. 25

Mr. E---a 75 year old man---was admitted from hospital following a left above-the-knee amputation caused by femoral embolism. Having been a very active man, and having lost his wife recently, this amputation led to a serious crisis of confidence in his abilities and in his future. His main difficulties were with mobility, transfers and coming to terms with the amputation itself. He also had serious doubts about coping at home independently.

Despite feeling negative about his future, Mr. E worked hard at his exercise programme and began to regain his self-confidence. The use of parallel bars, a wheelchair and a zimmer frame helped with his mobility. The rehabilitation team's objective was to encourage him to be independently mobile with a false limb. He was overwhelmed at his first visit home, and still felt a nursing home was his best option.

Client 25's (Mr. E's) ADL chart (Figure 5.1) indicates the progress that was made in transfers and the use of different catheter bags to help him regain independence. However, the 'beans' measure indicated that Mr. E continued to have mixed feelings about himself during his stay at Oakes Villa. The rehabilitation team was able to rebuild his confidence enough to discharge him to his own home after 6 weeks. He said that although he had been participating in the plans to discharge him back home, he never believed it would actually happen. One year after going home, Mr. E was still living independently and had restarted some of his hobbies.

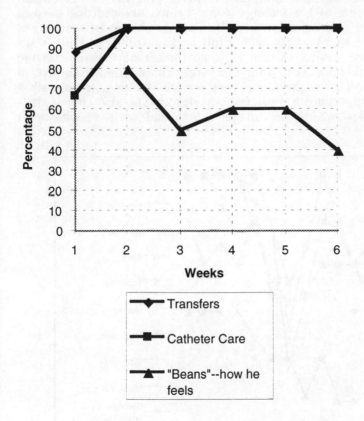

Figure 5.1   Progress chart of activities of daily living for client no. 25

Client no. 29

Mrs. D, aged   79 years, was admitted from a hospital following the effects of a stroke with right sided hemiplegia. Prior to this acute condition, she had reasonably good health, and enjoyed outdoor life. Whilst at the rehabilitation unit, Mrs. D was enabled to set her own goals and it was found that her main concern was her mobility.

Mrs. D's (Client 29 in Table 5.1) ADL chart (Figure 5.2) shows that she made considerable progress in her mobility and the use of a wheelchair, and became fully independent in dressing, washing, transfers, toileting, medication, getting in and out of bed, and the use of the kitchen for drinks/snacks. She fell ill during weeks 6 and 7 and suffered some setbacks, but continued to make progress in subsequent weeks. The measure of her feelings using 'beans' showed that she was also feeling more positive about herself. She was able to be discharged to her own home in 13 weeks, with a full package of three daily visits from a home care service, as well as some further day sessions at the rehabilitation unit. One year after discharge, she continued to live at home with support from the home care service, and is able to walk a little but continues to use her electric wheelchair. She also attends day-care every Sunday where she can get a bath and socialise with other people.

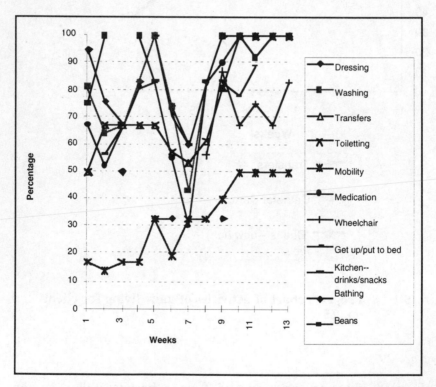

Figure 5.2 Progress chart of activities of daily living for client no. 29

Client no. 51

Mrs. M---an 84 year old lady---was admitted from a hospital, following the effects of a stroke with left sided hemiplegia. Her eyesight had also deteriorated following the stroke.

Mrs. M's (Client 51) ADL chart (Figure 5.3) shows that she made considerable progress in mobility, transfers, dressing, medication, and the use of the kitchen for drinks/snacks, although this progress was interrupted for two weeks (weeks 6 and 7) when she was readmitted to hospital. Initially, she was quite keen to return to her own home, and had a number of successful home visits. However, upon the advice of a family friend, Mrs. M decided that she would go into a nursing home, even though the rehabilitation workers' assessment was that she had made enough progress to live independently.

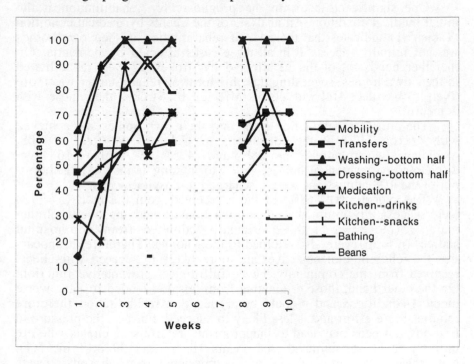

Figure 5.3   Progress chart of activities of daily living for client no. 51

Findings from outcome indicators

Based on single-case evaluation methodology involving the use of ADL charts and other assessment data, Table 5.1 indicates that, out of the total 106 clients where the outcome measures were used, 88 (83%) made progress with their daily living skills during their stay at the unit, 8 deteriorated, and there was no change in 6 clients. No measures were used with 2 clients, one of whom was too ill to enable proper assessments, and the other had not been there long enough before the end of this evaluation period.

An analysis of the 106 clients (Table 5.1) indicates that 34 were male and 72 (68%) female, with an age range of 48-94, and an average age of 78.8 years. The average age of the clients discharged to destinations other than their own homes was 81.6, as compared to 77.9 for the clients rehabilitated in their own homes, indicating that age itself was only marginally significant as a characteristic of those more likely to be successfully rehabilitated.

One significant factor in the prognosis for rehabilitation is the initial medical condition. An analysis of the clients by medical condition (Table 5.1) indicates that the goal of rehabilitation in their own homes was not initially successful in all three cases affected by dementia. On the other hand, out of the 32 affected by strokes, 22 were rehabilitated in their own homes, suggesting that this form of rehabilitation was more likely to be successful with clients affected by strokes than those with dementia.

The aim of rehabilitation back into their own homes was achieved with 79 (or 73%) of the admissions to Oakes Villa (total of 108, including two re-admissions 28b and 47b). A further 16 were discharged to residential homes, and 4 to nursing homes. Altogether, 9 out of the 108 admissions were discharged to hospital wards.

The majority (i.e., 68%) of those received from hospitals (n = 73) were successfully returned to their own homes; and the overwhelming majority (i.e. 83%) of those originally admitted from non-hospital sources (n = 35) were also returned to their homes. Therefore, it appears that the rehabilitation objectives are more likely to succeed with clients received from the community, hence fulfilling a preventative function. On the other hand, those originating from hospital tended to have worse medical conditions and it could be argued that rehabilitation therefore requires more effort and is less likely to succeed. Further, the pressure to free hospital beds may lead to inappropriate referrals of clients who are unlikely to be rehabilitated (see clients 18, 37 and 39 in Table 5.1). Nevertheless, 50 out of the 73 admissions from hospitals were rehabilitated in their own homes, indicating that the rehabilitation unit was effective in fulfilling its aims with the majority of such clients.

During the period of the research (June 1995 to March 1997), 89 people discharged from the unit were followed up six months after discharge, and it was found that 58 were continuing to live independently in the community, therefore adding weight to the conclusion that the unit has been largely effective in developing and fostering independent living with the majority of clients.

Table 5.1   Client input and output variables

Key for Activities of Daily Living (ADL) column:

I = evidence of progress in majority of variables
D = deterioration in majority of variables
N = no change in majority of variables
? = data not available

Other abbreviations:

CVA = strokes
COAD = chronic obstruction of airways disease
UTI = urinary tract infection
rescare = residential care
nurs.h = nursing home

hosp = hospital
com = admitted from own homes in community
dec'd = deceased
Blank spaces in the follow-up column = clients not yet followed up

No.	M/F	Age	Condition	Admitted From	ADL	Discharged To	Follow-up
1	f	76	Septicaemia	com	I	home	dec'd
2	f	76	Neglect	com	I	rescare	home
3	m	67	Dementia	hosp	N	hosp	home
4	f	85	Frailty	hosp	D	nurs.h	nurs.h
5	m	73	Fractures	hosp	I	home	home
6	f	67	Renal	hosp	I	home	home
7	f	86	CVA	hosp	I	rescare	rescare
8	m	87	Emphys	com	I	home	dec'd
9	f	83	frailty	hosp	I	home	home
10	f	83	CVA	com	I	home	home
11	m	73	angina	com	I	home	home
12	f	81	fractures	hosp	I	home	home
13	f	83	Parkinson's	com	I	home	home
14	m	65	CVA	hosp	I	home	home
15	f	94	CVA	rescare	N	home	home
16	f	93	fractures	com	N	home	home
17	f	62	CVA	hosp	I	home	home
18	f	50	N-H Lymphoma	hosp	I	hosp	home
19	f	67	Colorectos-copy	com	I	home	home
20	f	80	CVA	hosp	?	hosp	dec'd
21	m	87	CVA	hosp	I	home	home
22	m	79	fractures	hosp	I	home	home
23	f	90	fractures	hosp	I	home	home
24	f	92	immobility	com	I	home	home
25	m	75	amputation	hosp	I	home	home
26	m	78	CVA	hosp	I	home	home
27	f	94	immobility	com	I	home	home
28	f	86	fractures	hosp	I	home	rescare
28b	f	86	fractures	hosp	I	rescare	rescare
29	f	79	CVA	hosp	I	home	home
30	f	85	transfers	hosp	I	hosp	nurs.h
31	f	71	amputation	hosp	I	hosp	nurs.h
32	f	79	dementia	hosp	D	hosp	dec'd

No.	M/F	Age	Condition	Admitted From	ADL	Discharged To	Follow-up
33	f	85	arthritis	com	I	home	home
34	m	78	dementia	com	I	rescare	rescare
35	f	94	falls	hosp	I	rescare	rescare
36	f	80	fractures	hosp	I	home	home
37	f	92	diab.CVA	hosp	D	nurs.h	dec'd
38	f	82	fractures	com	I	home	home
39	m	73	falls	hosp	D	hosp	rescare
40	f	78	CVA	hosp	D	rescare	rescare
41	m	74	CVA	hosp	I	home	home
42	m	75	incont and memory	com	I	home	home
43	f	74	COAD	hosp	I	home	home
44	f	81	fallsandCVA	com	I	home	rescare
45	m	73	COAD	hosp	I	home	home
46	f	72	arthritis	com	I	home	home
47	f	76	CVA	com	I	home	home
47b	f	76	fractures	hosp	I	home	home
48	f	90	CVA	hosp	D	rescare	dec'd
49	f	79	CVA	hosp	D	rescare	rescare
50	m	85	amputation	hosp	I	rescare	rescare
51	f	84	CVA	hosp	I	nurs.h	nurs.h
52	f	70	falls	com	I	home	home
53	f	76	falls	com	I	home	home
54	m	59	heart	hosp	I	home	dec'd
55	f	92	fracture	hosp	D	rescare	rescare
56	m	75	poor mobility	com	N	hosp	home
57	f	86	falls	hosp	I	home	dec'd
58	f	88	fracture	hosp	I	home	home
59	f	82	pain re mobility	com	I	home	home
60	m	78	CVA	hosp	I	home	home
61	f	81	fracture	hosp	I	home	home
62	f	85	laparotomy	hosp	I	home	home
63	m	79	neck operation	hosp	I	home	home
64	f	71	fracture	hosp	I	home	home
65	m	69	CVA	hosp	I	home	home
66	m	81	depression	hosp	I	home	home
67	m	83	septicaemia	hosp	I	home	dec'd
68	f	83	UTI	com	I	home	home
69	f	91	poly-gastrectomy	hosp	I	home	home
70	f	87	fracture	hosp	N	rescare	dec'd
71	f	81	amputation	hosp	I	rescare	rescare
72	f	84	CVA	com		rescare	rescare
73	f	86	depression	hosp	I	home	home
74	f	75	CVA	hosp	I	home	home
75	m	65	CVA and amputation	com	I	home	home
76	f	86	fracture	com	I	home	rescare
77	f	91	CVA	com	I	home	home
78	f	88	CVA	hosp	I	rescare	rescare
79	m	81	fracture	hosp	I	home	home
80	m	77	chest pains	hosp	I	home	dec'd
81	m	77	poor mobility	com	I	home	home
82	m	69	fall	hosp	N	home	home
83	m	53	depression	hosp	I	home	home
84	f	48	amputation	hosp	I	home	home
85	m	68	infection	hosp	I	home	home
86	m	76	CVA	com	I	rescare	rescare
87	f	88	CVA	hosp	I	home	
88	f	85	falls	home	I	home	
89	f	70	poor mobility	home	I	home	home

No.	M/F	Age	Condition	Admitted From	ADL	Discharged To	Follow-up
90	f	84	hip replacement	hosp	I	home	
91	f	70	pulmonary oedema	com	I	home	
92	m	72	fracture	hosp	I	home	
93	f	94	falls	home	I	rescare	
94	m	72	CVA	hosp	I	home	
95	f	78	CVA	hosp	I	home	
96	f	82	CVA	hosp	I	home	
97	m	74	CVA	hosp	I	home	
98	f	85	CVA	hosp	I	home	
99	f	83	fracture	hosp	I	home	
100	f	85	ca.colon	hosp	?	hosp	
101	m	73	COAD	com	I	home	
102	f	63	fracture	com	I	home	
103	f	83	CVA	hosp	I	home	
104	f	82	fracture	hosp	I	home	
105	f	75	fracture	hosp	I	home	
106	f	86	frailty	hosp	I	nurs.h	

The service users' and referrers' surveys

Limitations of client studies include problems with the concept of satisfaction, as it has been demonstrated that general satisfaction will be expressed by as many as 80 per cent of recipients (Cheetham et al 1992). Rees and Wallace (1982) cite client studies which found that clients' expressions of satisfaction did not necessarily imply that they felt helped or found the service to be useful. Allen, Hogg and Peace (1992) found that client studies with older people report levels of satisfaction which are misleadingly high, often reflecting the low expectations of clients receiving domiciliary and residential services.

Nevertheless, a study of user perception is an important part of the evaluation. 'Users have useful things to say about both their own experiences and the wider aspects of services: greater participation in service decisions and planning would both meet users' demands and produce more effective services' (Marsh and Fisher 1992, p. 9). In the practice of community care, the views of clients must be given an airing and taken seriously (Shemmings and Shemmings 1995). Client surveys are often used as the only source of data for evaluating community care projects, as in the evaluation of the Staying at Home Initiative in Wales (Phillips et al 1993).

In November 1996, a postal survey was carried out of service users who had been discharged from Oakes Villa up to that month (some had been discharged for more than a year). Excluding clients who were known to have passed away or were very ill in hospital during that month,   64 questionnaires were sent and 41 questionnaires were subsequently returned by service users, indicating a response rate of 65 per cent. Apart from the 41, one questionnaire was returned by the post office, as the service user had moved. There were 12 questions, each with a rating scale of 5 points (e.g. 1 = not at all to 5 = very much). In most cases, the majority of the responders selected (5), and only 3 selected (1), indicating that they were not helped at all in the process of rehabilitation. In answering the question 'How helpful was your stay at Oakes Villa in helping you to return home', 29 out of 41 chose points 4-5, indicating high levels of satisfaction, 6 were ambivalent, and 5 were negative. The responses to the questionnaire indicate that although the majority were satisfied with Oakes Villa and the outcomes achieved, there was a significant minority where outcomes were less successful.

The final question was an open-ended question, and more than a page was provided for a response. Out of the 41 questionnaires returned, 24 service users (and/or their relatives/carers) addressed the question, 'Finally, is there anything you feel could be changed or introduced to improve the service offered on the Unit? Please give us your ideas'. Some respondents used this opportunity to provide their perceptions at length; others gave short answers. All but one of the 24 responses were positive.

A questionnaire for referrers was prepared by the Oakes Villa Unit's staff in consultation with the author, and posted to all the social services and hospital staff who had referred clients to Oakes Villa in the period up to the end of January 1997. The distribution list included 23 referrers based in the local social services department's area teams and the local hospitals. It was found that one had left and another was on long-term sick leave; and therefore 21 out of the 23 received the questionnaires. 10 questionnaires were returned, with a response rate of 47 per cent which was reasonable response for a postal survey. The questionnaire consisted of both qualitative and quantitative questions. All 10 referrers who responded to the survey reported that the unit's services were largely appropriate; 9 reported that their clients had largely improved during their stay at the unit, and 8 reported that the outcomes were what they expected.

Findings from multi-method evaluation

The findings were obtained from a variety of sources, based on a multi-method evaluation of Oakes Villa Rehabilitation Unit. These methods include single-case evaluation of all 108 admissions in the period, a needs analysis, focus group meetings with staff to determine the process of rehabilitation, survey of service users, and a survey of referrers to the unit. Each of these approaches has its limitations. For example, in the use of single-case evaluation it has not been possible to make comparisons with other clients also subject of a community care assessment and not referred to the unit in the same period, or to use the Activities of Daily Living Scale before and after the unit's services have been provided. Therefore, given the spontaneous element in recovery, it is not possible to determine the exact value provided by the unit to the client's efforts to regain or to maintain independent living in their own homes. Similarly, an evaluation based on client perceptions also has its limitations, given the findings from research that a large majority report high levels of satisfaction. Nevertheless, when several evaluation methods are combined, and all the indicators of evaluation used are pointing in the same positive direction, than it is possible to draw inferences regarding the unit's effectiveness with greater confidence. All of these evaluation methods have provided considerable evidence of Oakes Villa Rehabilitation Unit's effectiveness in achieving positive outcomes with a large majority of clients. The findings from single-case evaluation are an important part of that body of evidence which informs the evaluation of practice effectiveness.

Limitations of single-case evaluation as applied in this study

The quarterly reports provided charts for all clients whose progress was systematically tracked in this way. However, as the measurement was started and finished at the same time as the rehabilitation programmes, it was not possible to make before-and-after comparisons, and therefore the only question addressed was whether progress was made or not during the client's stay at the unit. It was not possible to infer the extent to which the unit's services were actually responsible for the client's progress (Kazi 1997). A further complication is that maturation cannot be ruled out, as a criteria for admission at the unit was a positive prognosis for improvement following the period of acute illness or other problems, and in any case there was a spontaneous element in the recovery process.

A causal link between the unit's programme and its effects could have been provided with the use of experimental group designs, including the use of outcome measures for all clients subject of a community care assessment, and comparing progress made by those who were not admitted to the unit with those who did receive the unit's services. However, even if such larger efforts at evaluation were possible, intake variables would also need to be taken into account in both groups in order to ascertain the value provided by the unit's services to the clients' development of their living skills. Even with this experimental group design, the results would still be difficult to interpret because of the element of spontaneous recovery. For example, it has been found that most patients make some spontaneous improvement after a stroke. At the same time, a number of studies have noted the association of poor outcomes with patient characteristics such as age and cognitive impairment (Jeffery and Good 1995; Riddoch et al 1995). At the time of writing, it is recognised that, as yet no specific stroke rehabilitation therapy has been shown to be better than another (Johansson 1993), despite the use of randomised controlled trial (RCT) group designs in a number of studies.

It should be recognised that the single-case designs (B designs--see Chapter 2) used in this evaluation are very weak, as in all cases the measurements begin and end at the same time as the rehabilitation interventions, and therefore no comparisons can be made with baselines prior to intervention. However, when combined with the other quantitative and qualitative methods used in the evaluation of Oakes Villa Rehabilitation Unit, the single-case designs provide a useful dimension to the evaluation in systematically tracking client progress.

6 Advantages and Limitations of Single-Case Evaluation

A number of texts analyse the advantages and limitations of single-case designs (e.g. Bloom and Fischer, 1982; Bloom, Fischer and Orme 1995; Sheldon 1982b; Kazdin 1982; and Blythe 1995). The analysis in this chapter is also based on the experience of application in the studies described in the preceding chapters, as well as others also involving collaboration between the author and practitioners in social work and other related practice settings. Generally, six key advantages can be identified.

First, the use of the designs makes practice more effective by encouraging a systematic approach in the definition of target problems, identification of goals, selection of intervention procedures, and in monitoring outcomes. 'The ultimate goal of all forms of single system designs is to improve practice' (Bloom and Fischer 1982, p. 22). Blythe (1995) argues that goal setting receives more attention than it often does in routine practice because of the requirement that the targets for intervention (that is, the client's goals) must be selected and carefully specified. The clear identification of dependent (target) and independent (treatment) variables reduces confusion between the two, as practitioners often restate treatment interventions rather than consider goals of the treatment. This was apparent in the probation study (Chapter 4) where the only outcome indicator in some cases was the process of reporting for supervision, rather than indicators which reflected the specific objectives the probation officer and the client hoped to achieve from the reporting process. The single-case evaluation project helped the trainee probation officers to consider outcome measures which went beyond the process of reporting.

Second, the designs are tools for evaluation which can be built into practice without disruption, and can contribute to the emergence of the 'practitioner-researcher' (Sheldon 1982b, p. 137). There is no need to bring in outside researchers except in a consultative role in the initial stages. The methodology is relatively easy to understand, and can be used in the same time-frame as the needs of practice in seeing clients. The designs can guide the practitioner through the assessment and specification of a client's goals, implementation of interventions, and termination and follow-up. 'Although these are nothing more than phases of practice, applying the components of single-system designs to these phases provides a degree of structure and some additional tools to aid in the process' (Blythe 1995, p. 2165). The use of measurement strategies enhances the information gathering, e.g. obtaining information from multiple sources reduces bias, and applying principles of reliability in interviews enhances accuracy. The examination of data patterns resulting from the ongoing collection of assessment data helps practitioners to make decisions about treatment plans as well as about continuing, discontinuing, or revising intervention strategies. When goals are met sufficiently, termination may take place. Follow-up may be facilitated when assessment measurement strategies are applied to determine whether gains have been maintained. In the adult rehabilitation project (Chapter 5), the data from single-case evaluation helped in deciding when a person was ready to live independently, and the follow-up assessment provided useful information regarding longer term benefits from the rehabilitation process.

Third, the designs can evaluate particular casework, and encourage collaborative working between the practitioner and the client. The focus is on the individual client (or group, or system) and the research is used for the benefit of both the practitioner and the client. We 'come to understand our client's target problem better because we have to clearly define it for measurement purposes' (Nelsen 1988, p. 374). The practitioner is actually monitoring his or her ability to help clients achieve goals. At the same time, the client is involved throughout the assessment processes of identifying target problems and goals, and in evaluating progress as treatment plans are implemented. This type of collegial relationship promotes the client's engagement and involvement in treatment (Blythe 1995, p. 2166). This process is also helped by visual presentation of the assessment data. In all the studies described in Chapters 3, 4 and 5, this type of collaborative working was an important feature, and the practitioners reported this as one of the main advantages of single-case evaluation.

Fourth, with the exception of the A and B single phase designs, single-case designs facilitate the testing of hypotheses or ideas, addressing the causal question---to what extent was the intervention responsible for the change? Based on the principles of concomitant variation and/or of unlikely successive coincidences (see Chapter 2), it may be possible to evaluate whether the practitioner's intervention could be causally linked to the observed changes. In this way, the more powerful single-case designs can enable comparisons of the effectiveness of different interventions. The establishment of a causal link is not a fundamental requirement of single-case evaluation---only the specification of target problems and the use of repeated measures.

However, if baseline and post-intervention data are available through such repeated measurement, then it may also be possible to establish causal links in varying degrees between the intervention and its effects. In the studies reported in the school setting in Chapter 3, a number of designs which fell into place naturally enabled such inferences to be made. In the Fartown groupwork project, it was possible to plan the use of ABA designs in advance, and to draw appropriate conclusions regarding the link between the groupwork programme and the observed effects. In the probation and rehabilitation studies, the establishment of causal links was not an aim due to the difficulties in obtaining repeated baseline and follow-up measures.

Fifth, the designs provide a model for enhancing the accountability of practitioners. 'Systematic, consistent use of single system designs will allow practitioners, and agencies, to collect a body of data about the effectiveness of practice that provides more or less objective information about the success of our practice' (Bloom and Fischer 1982, p. 15). The use of the designs enable social work practice to be empirically based and empirically validated in some circumstances. The studies reported in this book enabled judgements to be made regarding the effectiveness of particular interventions or particular projects, based on empirical data from aggregations of the results from single-case designs. Single-case evaluation is a useful and relatively simple means of developing evidence-based practice.

Finally, single-case evaluation is one methodology that can be used alongside others, and provides an empirical dimension to the process of evaluation. The adult rehabilitation study (Chapter 5) is a good example of a pragmatic, multi-method approach within which single-case evaluation was able to make a significant contribution.

The limitations of single-case designs

Like any other type of methodology, single-case designs have their own limitations. The following are a summary of the limitations of single-case designs from a review of some of the main published texts (Bloom and Fischer 1982; Kazdin 1982; Nelsen 1988; Sheldon 1982b, 1983; Barlow and Hersen 1984; Kratochwill, 1978; Bloom, Fischer and Orme 1995):

Although single-case designs help practitioners to guide and monitor practice, they must never dominate the practice. This applies to research designs in general, and not just single-case designs. Practice considerations must over-ride research considerations in social work practice.

Causal relationships that may be established with one client may not be applicable to others, depending on the extent to which direct and/or systematic replication is possible. Therefore, it must not be assumed that because one intervention programme is found to be successful with one client, it must be so with another, unless systematic replication across clients is possible in the course of normal practice which allows such a hypothesis to be tested.

The designs may be restricted in the range of questions about intervention effects that can be adequately addressed. For example, it is not usually possible to evaluate the relative effectiveness of two intervention procedures with a single-case analysis, as they can be considered only in sequence with carry-over effects not accounted for. Furthermore, the interaction of intervention effects with client characteristics cannot be addressed in most circumstances, and therefore there is no systematic way of determining whether the intervention procedure was more or less effective as a function of the intervention or the particular characteristics of the subjects. Robinson, Bronson and Blythe (1988) found that some students had difficulties in using the designs in circumstances where their clients' situations were complex and unpredictable, and where the target problems included the clients' wider environments.

Withdrawal phases are common in some single-case designs, but this process may raise ethical questions on the desirability of ending a successful intervention procedure for research purposes. Furthermore, some procedures cannot be withdrawn once they have been applied. However, this limitation does not apply where designs are enabled to unfold naturally, as withdrawals would take place because of practice considerations. It is considered to be desirable in most cases to wait for stable patterns in baseline data but it may not be possible to delay formal intervention until such a pattern emerges. This problem may be resolved with the construction of a baseline retrospectively, but only if reliable data is available for this purpose.

Threats to internal validity can be controlled and reduced, but they cannot be completely eliminated. Therefore, it is important to recognise these limitations when conclusions are drawn regarding causal links.

Some limitations found in the studies

Any evaluation study in social work cannot be perfect; it can only partially reflect reality. Therefore, even when every effort is made to reflect reality as accurately as possible, there will always be limitations which should be identified at each stage. For example, in the studies reported in this book, first there is the possibility of various errors in measurement---a limitation that can be minimised but not eliminated. The use of single-case designs presupposes the application of valid and reliable measuring instruments. However, because of the complexities involved in human problems, it is virtually impossible to construct a perfect instrument. Errors in measurement, e.g. client reactivity, desire to impress, and leniency on the part of the observer, can be minimised but not eliminated. Therefore, a limitation of the studies in the preceding chapters is that the measures that were constructed---such as rating scales, anger thermometer, and so on---provide only an indication of changes in the target problems. In some extreme cases, errors may provide misleading information to clients and practitioners, confounding the answers to the evaluative question.

Second, it is not clear from the data the extent to which other services (e.g. the schools in Chapter 3 and the alcohol education projects in Chapter 4) were involved in the practitioners' interventions. This limitation has arisen in particular because the strategy of these studies (with the exception of the adult rehabilitation study in Chapter 5) had been to concentrate on operationalising target problems rather than on defining intervention programmes. To enable replication of successful interventions, it is necessary to operationally define the interventions. However, by its nature, single-case evaluation concentrates on effects rather than content of the interventions. This issue is addressed further in the foregoing chapters, but one way of dealing with this is the application of single-case evaluation alongside other methods, e.g. the focus group meetings with the adult rehabilitation staff which enabled an analysis of the rehabilitation process itself.

Third, single-case designs are suitable only where the practitioner's involvement is such that repeated measurements can be obtained, and therefore this methodology cannot evaluate the brief work (i.e., one contact with the client without the use of repeated measurement) that is also undertaken by social workers. For example, in the Kirklees Education Social Work Study (Chapter 3), in addition to the 83 cases included, there were a further 8 cases that could not be analysed as they involved one or two contacts with clients.

Finally, although the study's strategy was to be as unobtrusive as possible with regard to the on-going practice of social workers, the participating practitioners reported that the completion of the data forms for this study increased their paperwork, as these recordings were over and above the requirements of the agency's existing recording systems. This was not an issue in specific projects such as the adult rehabilitation project or the government funded truancy and behaviour projects as these evaluation procedures were built into the recording systems from the outset.

Flexibility in application

The earlier attempts at the use of single-case designs emphasised not only that all target problems must be operationalised in measurable terms, but also that measures with proven reliability must be used, e.g. standardised measures in Corcoran and Fischer (1987) to enable the search for causal links between the intervention and its effects. However, the social work practitioners found that these measures were not sufficient in reflecting the client problems they were helping with, and therefore a number of target problems could not be measured appropriately with such measures alone. Therefore this requirement was relaxed and the practitioners were encouraged and helped to create their own measures which they felt were more appropriate in their practice, even though this was at the cost of reduced reliability, and some measures did not have the authority as demonstrable referents of a problem, but only as mere indications of a problem. For example, in the studies reported in this book, the emphasis on reliability was an attempt to minimise errors and to obtain measurements of sense perceptions which were as accurate as possible, but this emphasis at the later stages did not imply that only measures of proven reliability should be used. On the contrary, a number of self-report measures were used where the starting point of reliability was lower, even though the practitioner was encouraged to enhance reliability as much as possible.

Second, the emphasis in the 1980s and early 1990s was on experimental designs, that is, withdrawal designs which enable repeated comparisons between the intervention and the non-intervention phases, in attempts to establish a causal link between the social work intervention and its effects. The purpose was to test the hypothesis that a particular intervention programme will cause an improvement in the client's target problems. The basis for this approach was that effectiveness research should restrict itself to methods that enable verification (or falsification) with the purpose of demonstrating efficacy not only in terms of reaching agreed goals, but establishing a cause and effect link between the intervention and its efficacy. Viewed in this way, the experiment (i.e., randomised controlled trials) becomes the ideal gold standard in a hierarchy of research methods, and the other methods lower down the hierarchy (such as single-case designs used here) seek to approximate the gold standard as far as possible, in other to isolate the effects of the intervention by controlling for extraneous variables that may confound the relationship between the intervention and its effects.

However, in these studies, the practitioners felt that it would not be ethical to enable the use of repeated withdrawals of interventions in order to test their effects, nor was it feasible as in their circumstances they were responding to the needs of their clients as well as the needs of the schools to ensure improved attendance of targeted pupils. Therefore, the strategy was changed to reflect the realities of the situation, and it was agreed that, provided the target problems were operationalised and measured repeatedly, the exact nature of the designs used---whether there were withdrawal phases or not---would be determined by the needs of practice. It was accepted that randomised controlled trials would have been a better methodology to use in order to establish a causal link of this type, but as the emphasis was on the integration of effectiveness methodologies into practice by the practitioners themselves, it was felt such group comparisons would not be feasible.

In the probation study (Chapter 4), the strategy reflected the limited purposes of the project in the probation service---the aim was to systematically track client progress, not to attribute a causal link between the probation supervision programme and the progress made by the client. This was an example of pragmatism---the author engaged in a partnership with the practitioners to identify the purpose of the effectiveness study, and used strategies that served that purpose, even if it was narrowly defined, and even if internal and/or external validity was weak. However, the selection and application of the design reflected the author's empirical practice paradigm at the time of the study. The main purpose identified, based on the needs of practice at the time, was for an effectiveness strategy that could enable a systematic tracking of client outcomes. In this example, effectiveness was defined narrowly as the achievement of agreed objectives, and performance measurement was used to indicate whether a Probation Order was effective or not in meeting its objectives. The research strategy used was based on single-case evaluation combined with some classificatory indicators. In this sense, the strategy used is part of the empirical practice movement within probation services (Macdonald 1994). However, the strategy falls well short of the gold standard of RCTs (Macdonald 1996), as the design used was pre-experimental, with no internal validity. Although the design was appropriate for the stated purpose of systematically tracking client outcomes, no causal link could be established between the Probation Order and the client's progress, as alternative explanations for the observed progress could not be ruled out.

A serious limitation of the studies reported in Chapters 3 and 4 was that the content of interventions was virtually ignored. The concentration was on the specification and measurement of target problems---or the targets of the intervention, but not on the nature of the intervention itself. How the particular intervention strategy was actually selected by the social worker was not part of the investigation; nor was there an emphasis on describing the intervention programme in the detail required for future replication. An attempt was made to encourage the practitioners to describe their interventions, but they tended to do this with the minimum description required in their routine recording systems.

From a critical theorist perspective (see Chapter 7), Shaw (1996) argues against a growing resurgence of empirical practice within the probation service. He criticises the 'what works' campaign (McGuire and Priestley 1995) as management by effectiveness; and as a pragmatist approach devoid of any ideology, simply advocating that probation officers should do whatever works. In other words, the content of practice is not addressed---but simply whether it works or not. This, indeed, was one of the limitations of the probation study described in Chapter 4.

The emphasis was not on developing the intervention strategies themselves, but it was hoped that if sufficient evidence was provided to indicate that the desired outcomes were not reached, then the social worker would change the actual strategies used. In practice, the intervention was seen as a static entity, and its content was virtually ignored.. This limitation is not just that of single-case evaluation---it is a feature of other methodologies also associated with the empirical practice perspective such as randomised controlled-trials. This particular limitation was addressed in the adult rehabilitation study by going outside of this paradigm and using additional methodologies. These issues are considered further in Chapter 7.

Critique of single-case evaluation

Single-case evaluation is one of the main methodologies used within the empirical practice perspective, and as such becomes part of any critique of this perspective, even though in this author's experience this methodology is versatile enough to be applied within any of the main contemporary evaluation research perspectives (see Chapter 7). From a critical theorist's perspective, Shaw (1996, 1998) outlines a number of arguments against the empirical practice approach in social work effectiveness research. First, it is not clear that empirical practice methods can be applied to all or even most of social work practice because of the complexities involved. Second, empirical practice tends to be reductionist and place demands of measurement which are incompatible with the realities and meanings of practice. Third, ethical issues, such as anti-discriminatory practice, have been given too little attention. Finally, single-case designs in particular were intrusive on practice, and although the threat of disruption of service may be marginal, it was not inconsequential. However, these criticisms are levelled not at the level of paradigmatic influences of empirical practice, but at the level of whether the methodology of single-case evaluation is appropriate for social work.

Empirical practice--or any other paradigm--should be seen for what it contributes to effectiveness research, and what its limitations actually are. Most arguments in British social work research circles, however, concentrate on methodological issues associated with particular methodologies---not the paradigms. In that light, the points raised by Shaw (1998), were responded to by Kazi (1998). This reply is based on the author's experience of applying single-case evaluation; these answers reflect the author's paradigm shifts to some extent, but they are responses at the level of methodological considerations in application to social work practice.

First, it is argued that it may not be possible to apply this approach to all or even most of social work. In fact, it is applied to much of social work practice. This author has worked with social workers and allied professions in education, probation, residential, adult rehabilitation, and child protection settings where empirical practice has been applied by fairly large numbers of social workers. However, a limitation of single-case evaluation is that it can be applied only in circumstances where repeated assessments can be made; therefore it is not suitable in 'one-off' sessions of work with clients.

Second, it is argued that the demands of measurement are incompatible with the realities and meaning of practice. The charge of reductionism is relevant, e.g. in the probation study (Chapter 4) where single-case designs provided evidence of progress but could not determine which factors in the clients' circumstances led to the progress that was achieved. A limitation of single-case evaluation is that it cannot address such wider questions; other methods can be used for this purpose. However, single-case evaluation should not be criticised for not helping in areas it is not designed to help---it is simply a verification (or falsification) procedure to determine if the client is making progress as desired.

Third, it is argued that ethical issues have been given too little attention because of the emphasis on measurable outcomes without consideration of the moral issues and values. The use of single-case evaluation alongside other methods in the evaluation of Oakes Villa Rehabilitation Unit (Chapter 5) demonstrates that empirical practice is not incompatible with the values of social work---it simply provides additional information to both the worker and client about the progress made to achieve the client's goals, and provides evidence of effectiveness of the social work intervention. The emphasis on measurement in both the probation and adult rehabilitation studies did not lead to a dependence on 'technical expertise' or 'performance culture' that Shaw fears---on the contrary, it complemented existing practice in such a way that partnership between worker and client was strengthened, with the client participating in the process of evaluation---one of the preconditions for anti-discriminatory, anti-oppressive practice. It should be acknowledged, though, that particularly in the probation study, there was a tendency to concentrate on measurable objectives (see Chapter 4), and in that sense single-case evaluation as a method (by itself) cannot address the content---and therefore ethics and values that are part of the content---of programmes.

Finally, the intrusion of research design was not as great as feared by Shaw in his fourth point---the procedures were integrated into practice in most cases, and practice unfolded as it would have done naturally. The 'marginal effect' on the services concerned was a focus on the objectives of the education social work, or of the probation order, or of the adult rehabilitation process---a focus which was welcomed by both the social workers and the clients.

Single-case evaluation cannot answer all the evaluation questions of social work practice, but it is a useful means for the systematic tracking of client progress. Therefore, it is not the only way to evaluate practice-- it is one of a wide range of methodologies available, including both qualitative and quantitative approaches. Single-case evaluation is one method that can be incorporated into social work practice to provide on-going evidence of effectiveness---it can be used as part of a pragmatic, methodological-pluralist framework, to address the complex evaluation questions that are relevant to the needs of social work practice. This methodology can also be used as part of a critical theorist perspective, or even as part of a scientific realist perspective---these issues are considered in the next chapter.

7 Contemporary Perspectives in Effectiveness Research

The pressures on social work practice to demonstrate its effectiveness have continued to grow in the last two decades in England. Effectiveness research is one way to make social programmes accountable and to enable politicians, agencies and practitioners to make hard choices in the allocation of scarce resources. There are two main purposes of effectiveness practice research---providing evidence of the worth of social work practice, and striving to improve practice itself to respond to the changing needs and contexts. Whether emphasis is placed on one or the other or on both of these purposes depends on the paradigmatic influences that are inherent in the effectiveness inquirer's activities. The role of particular methodologies such as single-case evaluation---how it is used, and for what purpose---depends upon the perspective of the enquirer. This chapter provides a brief analysis of the main perspectives in effectiveness research in the context of the complexities of social work practice, and the contribution single-case evaluation can make within each of these perspectives.

Complexities of social work practice

The Central Council for Education and Training in Social Work (CCETSW 1989, p. 8) defines social work practice as:

> an activity which enables individuals, families and groups to identify personal, social and environmental difficulties adversely affecting them. Social work enables them to manage these difficulties through supportive, rehabilitative, protective or corrective action.

Social work practice takes place in an open system, usually working with the social work client in a holistic way; and therefore it cannot operate without taking into account the person's environment or context. Social work interventions usually take place at the interface of the individual and social, where multiple factors and influences are continuously at work. Therefore, in such circumstances, the most a scientific inquirer can strive for is an explanation which can only approximate the realities of practice, and the best that can be achieved is probabilistic knowledge.

Figure 7.1 attempts to illustrate the complexities of social work practice. Effectiveness questions may include ethics and the value-base, the processes (including the process of assessment, the content of intervention and the social work theory on which the practice strategy is based), and the outcomes of social work practice, as the first dimension. These factors may need to be addressed from the perspectives of service users, social workers, managers, other professionals, and significant others relevant to the practice--which constitute the second dimension. Finally, both of these dimensions are underpinned by the context in which social work takes place, including the influences from the underlying mechanisms, structures and systems. Figure 7.1 is, of course, a very crude attempt to illustrate the complexities, because each of these dimensions, and the factors within each, are in a continuous state of flux---and cannot be characterised as blocks with distinct boundaries.

The complexities of practice are such that outcome data alone may not provide the relevant perspectives on whether the outcomes achieved were in fact desirable given the clients' circumstances within the context of practice. In order to develop more effective practice, it is helpful to know not only the extent to which client objectives were achieved, but also which process was effective and under what circumstances. The context of practice is fluid and inherently unpredictable; at the same time, failure to address context renders any explanation at best incomplete. For example, if the effectiveness strategy addresses both the practice and perspective dimensions at the surface without digging deeper into contexts, and even if such scrutiny finds that the desirable outcomes were achieved with most service users (and even if a causal link between process and outcome can be found), such an explanation will be incomplete because it will not address why the programme was successful with some clients and not with others, and future successes cannot be guaranteed. The researcher can either gather data at the surfaces alone, or attempt to dig deeper into the contexts. The dimensions of practice that are targeted by the researcher, and the extent to which the complexities are addressed, depend upon a) the paradigmatic perspective of the researcher, and b) the extent to which the particular perspective enables the researcher to address these complexities.

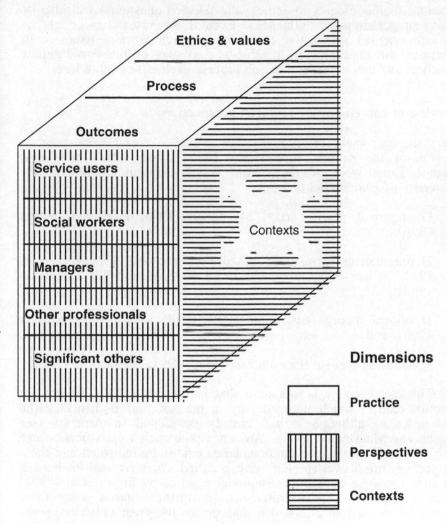

Figure 7.1   Dimensions of practice

Effectiveness research, or indeed any other type of research, cannot be methodology-driven to the exclusion of paradigmatic influences, as the ontology and epistemology of the inquirer will profoundly affect what is researched and how. The choice of effectiveness questions (for example whether effectiveness of social work practice is seen in a holistic way or whether emphasis is placed on processes, or on outcomes, or on user or other perspectives, and even decisions regarding the feasibility of particular methodologies to address the selected questions) will also be subject of paradigmatic influences. Even if the researcher adopts an outcome oriented perspective that does not include value-issues in its repertoire, the inquirer's own value-base is part of the paradigmatic influence, and therefore the research process itself is not value-free.

A review of contemporary research perspectives

There are four main perspectives that influence social work practice research at the present time (Kazi 1998a), and which have also influenced the work of the Centre for Evaluation Studies at the University of Huddersfield:

1) empirical practice (e.g. Macdonald 1996, Kazi and Wilson 1996);

2) pragmatism or methodological-pluralism (e.g. Cheetham et al 1992, Fuller 1996, Fuller and Petch 1995, Kazi 1998, Cheetham 1998);

3) critical theory (e.g. Shaw 1996, 1998; Everitt and Hardiker 1996); and

4) scientific realism (Pawson and Tilley 1997a, 1997).

This classification is similar to that in Trinder (1996), except for scientific realism which emerged only in the last year in British social work research, although it had already developed in America (see Anastas and MacDonald 1994). Any attempt at such a classification can only be a crude attempt, as the boundaries tend to be indistinct and these perspectives often overlap {e.g. what is called scientific realism here is placed in the same category as empirical practice by Fraser et al (1991) under the term of post-positivism}. A further reason why these boundaries are not so clear-cut is that, unlike the great epistemological debate in America, in the main these four perspectives share the same ontology. As for which perspective is dominant in practice, Trinder (1996) notes that most Department of Health funded research is in fact pragmatist, based on non-experimental quantitative methodologies including surveys---a view also corroborated by American reviews of the products of social work research (see Fraser et al 1991).

The contemporary paradigms in social work research are a reflection of the debates in the philosophies of social science. The basis for these controversies lies in the demise of foundationism (i.e., the certainty of knowledge obtained from the senses) on which the earlier versions of positivism was based. In the earlier part of this century, the positivist paradigm was dominant in academia, along with the positions that positive knowledge was based on causal laws of phenomena derived from observation, and that the world could be observed as it was through the senses. Propositions which could not be tested or verified---i.e., those beyond sensory experience---were deemed to be meaningless. However, Karl Popper, Kuhn and others challenged the view that knowledge could be based on 'facts' as absolute truths. Scientific knowledge could not achieve absolute certainty in terms of facts, as observation was both theory-laden and value-laden; and at best scientific knowledge was probabilistic knowledge---what is known today is an approximation of truth, and such approximations change and develop as progress is made. There is no certain way to compare a theory to theory-neutral reality, and therefore, the problem of science or knowledge cannot finally be resolved (Manicas 1987, p.263-4). The world cannot be known as it is, because it is mediated by socially and historically constituted practices. Therefore, choice between competing theories (e.g. theories of social support) depends upon a mixture of objective and subjective factors of shared and individual criteria amongst those making the selections. In other words, no research process can be perfect---there are always limitations, and the findings from research can be true only until further notice.

A number of anti-positivist paradigms emerged from this realisation, holding different ontological and epistemological positions---and these are also reflected in the contemporary publications in British social work research. If the philosophy of science holds that truth and certainty are not attainable, then at the level of ontology (i.e. theories about the nature of being), one has to make choices---either one takes the position that there is a reality out there in the world, and that one can use the reflection of this reality as a standard to strive at (no matter how imperfect); or one can take it to its ultimate conclusion, that there is no reality which can be used as a standard, and therefore there are many truths which are all equally true even if they are contradictory. The first position is known as realism; the second is that of some (not all) interpretevist approaches such as constructivism. Constructivism holds that realities exist in the form of multiple mental constructs and there is no reality external to these constructs (Guba 1990, p. 27). However, in England such non-realist perspectives tend to be under-represented in practice research.

Empirical practice movement

Empirical practice tends to be associated with positivism (Thyer 1993a), and it is within this perspective that single-case-evaluation as a methodology was born. However, it is not possible to describe positivism in the sense of a single paradigm or a single description which captures the essence of positivism enough to satisfy even all of those researchers who admit to following positivism. Outhwaite (1987 pp. 6-7) notes at least twelve varieties of positivism, and therefore any single description of positivism as a paradigm will not be able to do full justice to all the variants. In social work circles, positivism is identified with methodology rather than a perspective; and those who promote, say randomised controlled trials or single-case designs, or those who want to apply outcome measures to effectiveness in order to provide evidence for testing social work interventions---tend to be associated with a single entity called positivism.

A drawback of the failure to identify the particular ontology or epistemology of the 'positivists' is that, in the great epistemological debate, they tend to be tarred with the same brush---and at times tarred with the most extreme version of positivism that an anti-positivist can find. An example from the American epistemological debate is Tyson's (1992) assertion that all proponents of empirical practice in social work assume that observation is theory-free. Within the epistemological debate, an assumption is made that empirical practice in social work is associated with foundationist positivism which believes in the certainty of objective knowledge as true reflections of reality, or in the certainty of causal links between phenomena. In fact, the empirical practice movement is based on a realist ontology---and not foundationism. Fortunately, the British social work version of the debate tends to be more realistic---for example, Shaw (1996, p. 109) does draw a line between the various forms of positivism that he criticises (largely from the standpoint of critical theory), and Popperian anti-deterministic objectivity, and also (rightly, in this author's view) cautions social workers from confining neo-positivism and/or Popper to the dustbin. Also from a critical theoretical standpoint, Everitt and Hardiker (1996, p. 51) criticise empirical practice, but accept that randomised controlled trials may be useful in some circumstances.

Empiricism is more than simply relying upon evidence from the senses. Empirical practice is based on verifiable, systematic observations subject to 'some evidentiary standards of proof' (Thyer and Wodarski 1998, p. 2). If we define empirical practice in terms of an emphasis on verifiable or evidence-based outcomes, then in British social work practice research there appears to be two main movements associated with the empirical practice perspective. First, there is the promotion of single-case evaluation procedures which could be used by practitioners to ascertain the effects of their practice through the measurement of client outcomes. This author's work to promote the use of single-case evaluation by social work practitioners in a variety of settings has been reported in the preceding chapters and elsewhere (Kazi 1996, 1997 and 1998). Second, there is the promotion of randomised controlled trials (RCTs) which can establish causal links between the social work programmes and their effects with greater confidence. An example of this trend are the recent publications of the biggest children's charity in Britain, namely Barnardos (Oakley 1996, Macdonald 1996).

The contribution of empirical practice

In the 1970s and 1980s, most effectiveness strategies were dominated by the empirical practice or outcome-oriented approaches. That is because a) the empirical practice perspective was the first to recognise the need for providing evidence of effectiveness and to develop effectiveness strategies (e.g. by drawing a distinction between the intervention and its effects); and b) its focus on outcomes lends itself to an emphasis on effectiveness in the (albeit narrow) sense of social work practice causing a desired effect, and the attempt to test an intervention's effects. The anti-positivist approaches tended to be pre-occupied with describing or exploring questions of process and context which were felt to be more important than providing evidence of effectiveness. In the earlier stages, the epistemological debate within social work research circles centred around whether it was possible or even desirable to address effectiveness questions given the complexities of social work (Sheldon 1978, Jordan 1978); latterly (although the earlier questions are by no means resolved), this debate has moved on to how effectiveness questions could be addressed, to the extent that researchers critical of empirical practice are attempting to develop alternative effectiveness strategies (Shaw 1996, Everitt and Hardiker 1996).

An important contribution of empirical practice is the drawing of a distinction between the social work programmes and their effects. Going back to Figure 7.1, empirical practice enables a distinction to be made between the processes and the outcomes of social work, in the realm of practice (i.e., the top or surface of the box). It also attempts to link the process and outcomes in ways that enable, at the very least, some evidence of progress by which the effects of the process could be judged; and at most, enables a causal link to be made between the process and the outcome to strengthen such judgements. In general there is a common belief that scientific procedures such as the hypothetico-deductive approach can be applied to social work practice, and that knowledge is based on observable phenomena that can provide the evidence of outcomes. For example, Martin and Kettner (1996, p. 3), note that 'performance measurement incorporates a focus on outcomes (i.e. the results, impacts, and accomplishments) of human service programs' (see also Bryman 1988, Thyer 1993). Hypotheses to be tested may be formulated either as 1) causal connections between variables, or simply as 2) that the introduction of an independent variable (e.g. the intervention) would lead to changes in the dependent variable (e.g. client objectives). Hypotheses of either formulation are then empirically tested in the form of outcome measures which provide evidence. Single-case evaluation is used typically to track client progress in order to address the latter type of hypotheses.

Limitations of empirical practice

Empirical practice researchers acknowledge its limitations. For example, in the application of the gold standard of RCTs, there are technical limitations---no-treatment control groups or random allocation to groups may not be possible, and the trials may be too expensive; but, it is argued, RCTs potentially offer something others cannot: 'maximum security in results' (Macdonald 1996, p. 23).

At the lower end of the hierarchy of positivist methods, Kazi, Mantysaari and Rostila (1997) also acknowledge the limitations of single-case designs: a) this methodology was a verification procedure and could not determine what the intervention itself should be; b) because of the requirement for repeated measurement, it could not be applied to social work that involved a single contact with the client; c) they could not represent the full perspective of any party, the desirability of the intervention, or the context of practice; d) it cannot assess issues of ethics and values; and e) it is pre-experimental and therefore cannot establish a causal link with confidence as the RCTs can.

More generally, a major limitation of empirical practice is that there is a tendency to concentrate on effects, to a virtual exclusion of consideration of the content of the intervention that is tested, as explained by the philosopher Medawar (1982, p. 135):

> The weakness of the hypothetico-deductive system, in so far as it might profess to offer a complete account of the scientific process, lies in its disclaiming any power to explain how hypotheses come into being.

Even if randomised controlled trials are used, this central limitation remains. Oakley (1996) provides examples of RCTs, which whilst providing a robust examination of the effects of a social programme, also fail to address the content of the programme itself. For instance, RCTs were used to test the effectiveness of social support for pregnant women. Oakley provides an extensive analysis of the types of outcomes and the characteristics of the random groups, but there is extremely little information about the nature of the social support programme itself, nor is there any evidence of a dynamic approach to the development of the nature of social support. This limitation is not just a question of methodology that needs to be addressed in future applications. Whilst some improvements could be made in future applications, the central issue here is one of the paradigm--the ontology and epistemology of the inquirer using the methodologies. This limitation of virtually ignoring content is at the heart of the empirical practice paradigm. A further limitation is that contexts are also virtually ignored---because the contribution made is partial rather than holistic, concentrating on the outcomes at the surface of the box in Figure 7.1, empirical practice approaches are limited in addressing the full complexities of social work practice.

Pragmatism or methodological-pluralism

Fuller (1996, p. 59) outlines three basic elements of the methodological-pluralist or pragmatic approach:

- the suspension of not-to-be-resolved philosophical conundra in the interests of getting on with the job.

- making contextual judgements about the trade-off between what might be desirable, by way of research design, and what is feasible. This can include what may seem to some like a dangerously impure regard for credibility of certain research methods with intended audiences.

- abandoning the search for the evaluator's stone which would turn all to the gold of irrefutable scientific proof.

Central to the pragmatist position is the desire to 'get on with the job' of effectiveness research---Fuller's position is to place the needs of practice first, thereby considering the epistemological debates to be a waste of time as the issues debated around the comparison of theory with theory-neutral reality cannot be resolved. This author, too, reflected the same 'getting on with the job' trend in the paper presented at Stockholm (Kazi 1997a). These positions have led to a charge that pragmatism is essentially an anti-intellectual trend in social work research, and that it is an 'unashamedly empirical approach to research, steering a course between the scientific empiricism of the positivist project and the messier politicised approach to research of participative/critical researchers' (Trinder 1996). It has also been attacked as 'anything goes' (Macdonald 1996). In fact, the advent of the pragmatic approach to mixing methods is a consequence of the epistemological debate, in the sense that this debate has helped to a) recognise the limitations of the methods associated with each paradigm, and b) enable the realisation that qualitative methods are acceptable and can be combined with quantitative methods to present a more comprehensive approximation of reality. Ontologically, pragmatists tend to draw the line at relativism, and therefore, at least at the level of ontology, it is not 'anything goes'.

Cheetham et al (1992, p. 20) describe this approach as 'eclectic, not wedded to a single alliance', and explain that because of the 'diversity, occasional elusiveness and the generally shifting sands of social policy in action', adherence to a single approach 'would risk leaving much social work activity unresearchable'. Feasibility is an important factor in the selection of methods---one should begin with the evaluation questions and then select a method (or a combination of methods) which can be applied appropriately to address the relevant questions. Typical methods are secondary analyses (study of records), monitoring devices (some measures), questionnaires, interviews, scales and schedules, observation and diaries with a largely quantitative base, but with some efforts at gaining qualitative insights. Single-case evaluation is not included in the methods described in Fuller and Petch (1995); however, the mixing of methods in effectiveness studies as reported in Kazi (1997, 1997a and 1998) and in Chapter 5 where single-case evaluation was combined with other methods in the evaluation of adult rehabilitation programmes, was influenced by the pragmatic approach advocated by colleagues at the University of Stirling in Scotland.

The empirical practice distinction between process and outcomes is accepted, but there are various ways of addressing the connection between them. 'Indeed, it can be forcibly argued that a sophisticated understanding of social work, and indeed all the human services, should now be informed by these two rather different kinds of knowledge---in jargon, about outcomes and processes---and seek to connect them' (Cheetham 1998, pp. 9-10). Within this perspective, for example, single-case evaluation or randomised controlled trials would not be seen as an empirical revolution, but as one of a range of equally valid methods available to evaluate social work practice. The limitations of each methodology would be recognised, and other methods would be used to address the questions that any one methodology was unable to address.

For example, one of the main weaknesses of the single-case evaluation studies (Chapters 3 and 4) was that the focus was on measures of effectiveness rather than on the actual content of the social work programmes used. In the latter adult rehabilitation study Chapter 5), content was an important question for inquiry, and qualitative methodologies (e.g. focus groups influenced by critical theory) were used to explore the nature of the social programmes---the actual services provided, and the values and theories underpinning them. The richness of the data obtained through the use of both positivist and naturalistic approaches enabled the author to draw more informed inferences regarding the project's effectiveness.

Advantages and limitations of pragmatism

Going back to Figure 7.1, through combining various approaches, the pragmatist takes on board the advantages of empirical practice and attempts to compensate for its limitations through triangulation. The definition of effectiveness is still in the empirical practice sense of drawing a distinction between the social work intervention and its effects, and effects are empirically tested with the use of both quantitative and qualitative methodologies. At the same time, the content is analysed with greater insight. In this way, methodological-pragmatism can dig deeper into the complexities of social work practice---more objective outcome data is combined with more subjective perspectives of all the parties concerned, and the context is also taken into account to some extent if desired. Therefore, in Figure 7.1, the pragmatic approach of realist methodological-pluralism can not only establish connections between process and outcomes of practice, but also the ethics and values, and the perceptions of all the parties involved. In addition, it digs into the context a little deeper than the empirical practice approach.

A limitation of methodological-pragmatism is that it may concentrate on the needs of stakeholders or the needs of practice, and therefore fail to capture the effectiveness of a social work programme in a holistic way. This is particularly so if the inquirer tends to become essentially methodological-driven or considers feasibility to be the main criteria. In terms of its explanatory powers, methodological-pragmatism may concentrate on the expressed needs of the participants in negotiating questions of inquiry, and fail to capture the main features of the mechanisms which influence the effectiveness of programmes in an open system. These pitfalls will ensure that although the explanation of reality may be improved when compared with empirical practice, the effectiveness of practice will be apprehended at best only partially. Furthermore, like empiricist researchers, pragmatic researchers tend to make judgements about past practice rather than developing future practice.

Critical theorist perspective

The critical theorist paradigm of research is advocated in British social work by Shaw (1996) and Everitt and Hardiker (1996). It is politically-oriented inquiry which includes movements aimed at the emancipation of oppressed people, including feminist, neo-Marxist and other forms of participatory inquiry. 'Evaluating in practice...is not about reflective rigour in empowering but concerns a practice which is legitimated only through the test of whether it empowers and emancipates...Effectiveness is truth' (Shaw 1996, p. 110). The task of the inquiry is to raise people (mainly service users, and to some extent also practitioners---but, it is implied, not managers) from the various forms of false consciousness they have due to their oppressions, to a level of true consciousness which helps to emancipate oppressed people and enables them to transform their situation. Therefore, the ontology is by definition critical realist ('true' consciousness), coupled with a subjectivist epistemology which relates the inquiry's activities to the values of the inquirer (Guba 1990).

Methodologically, the critical theorists take a dialogic approach that aims to rally participants and raise their consciousness of reality in order to achieve desired changes. This dialogic process helps achieve greater self-knowledge and self-reflection in order to transform people towards greater autonomy and responsibility, hence linking both theory and practice. Understanding comes by change and change comes by understanding. The methodologies incorporate both empirical analyses and historical hermeneutics; but hard data is not considered to be any better than soft data. Surveys tend not to be used, as they do not reflect the full intents and purposes of people; therefore the critical theorist's preference is for qualitative approaches that enable the inquirer to dig deeper into the underlying values, meanings and interpretations of the participants (Popkewitz 1990). The ontology is realist also in the sense that issues of methodology are in part related to a historical context, concerning power and control in society; therefore the scientific process interacts with the realities of the historical conditions in which it works. The process of scientific enquiry is not technical or procedural, but is embedded in values, ethics, morality and politics.

On the basis of critical theory, Everitt and Hardiker (1996) suggest that effectiveness research should enable a dialogue between users and the organisation, as well as between social workers and the organisation, to enhance their feelings of being valued and to strive for high standards of good practice which include a strong emphasis on issues of power, powerlessness, race, gender, disability and social class. The purpose is to make judgements about value and effecting change in the direction of the 'good'. Critical theory helps in locating people's perceptions within the social, political and economic contexts, particularly in relation to structural oppression and discrimination.

Shaw (1996, pp. 115-6) combines critical theory with Popperian falsifiablity (as well as other influences) suggesting the following approach to evaluation of practice:

- participatory evaluating with service users

- reflecting on tacit knowing-in-practice

- describing practice in ways that render access to its strengths and weaknesses feasible

- mutual reflexivity of both practitioner and service user

- legitimation through falsifying and grounded plausibility.

Although critical theorists are inherently suspicious of any methodology based on quantitative or hard data, single-case evaluation can contribute to participatory evaluation with service users, and also inform the mutual reflexivity of both practitioner and service user, by providing evidence of progress against objectives agreed with the service users. By enabling service users to evaluate their own progress through self-report measures, this methodology is not incompatible with the goal of emancipation---indeed, it can contribute to this process.

Contributions and limitations of critical theory

Critical theorists place the emphasis on the raising of consciousness and the emancipation of oppressed client groups that receive the service of social work. To the extent that social work practice can achieve this, then it is judged as good---and in this context, effectiveness is truth, and is arrived at through focus groups, life history work and a mix of methods that do not exclude quantitative measures but prefer qualitative approaches. As far as evidence based practice is concerned, the emphasis is placed on the perspectives and insights of the participants. Effectiveness research is a contributor to this process of striving for emancipation and true consciousness, as well as enabling judgements to be made as to whether the practice is good. In this way, critical theory goes further than empirical practice in addressing the content of practice, the ethics and values, the multiple perspectives, and to some extent the contexts as well.

Critical theorist researchers not only have the advantages of the realist methodological-pragmatic approach, but also provide an additional emphasis on the perceptions of users and practitioners. They emphasise ethics, values and moral issues, and attempt to make such issues part of the process and outcome of social work practice. When combined with methodological-pragmatism, critical theory can add a richer dimension to effectiveness research, as this author found in an evaluation of a mental health advocacy service. Standardised outcome measures from Fischer and Corcoran (1994) were combined with semi-structured surveys and focus groups based on a critical theorist standpoint, providing a richer account of the process of advocacy, its effects, and the perceptions of the participants; at the same time, the process of research itself participated in the raising of consciousness of the mental health service users. In the adult rehabilitation study (Chapter 5), the critical theorist perspective was adopted with the use of focus groups to investigate content of the rehabilitation process, and single-case evaluation was used within a largely pragmatist framework to achieve a richer and more holistic evaluation.

A limitation of critical theory is that it tends to concentrate on the needs of stakeholders and their perceptions, and therefore fails to capture the effectiveness of a social work programme in a holistic way. There is a tendency to be suspicious of attempts to measure effects of services---this in part explains Shaw's (1998) heavily critical stance towards single-case evaluation even where this methodology is no more than a systematic tracking of client outcomes. This one-sidedness means that critical theorist researchers will not begin with a holistic perspective, thereby failing to capture all the dimensions of social work practice as illustrated in Figure 7.1.

The scientific realist perspective

There is a new perspective called scientific realism (or just realism, fallibilistic realism, and even postpositivism), which is inclusive of all other perspectives that share the same ontology. In other words, it excludes only foundationist positivism (which holds that reality can be apprehended as it is) and relativism (perspectives that hold that as there is no certain truth, differing perceptions in the minds of people are all true--e.g. constructivism and postmodernism). Therefore, it is inclusive of empirical practice, pragmatic and critical theorist perspectives.

The term fallibilistic realism was first suggested by Donald Campbell in a personal communication (Manicas and Secord, 1983); and it is used by Anastas and MacDonald (1994) who were the first to introduce this perspective in social work effectiveness research (however, if we include texts in the Finnish language then Professor Mikko Mantysaari, University of Tampere, Finland wrote about scientific realism in relation to social work a few years before Anastas and MacDonald). This perspective is also known by other terms, such as transcendental realism, referential realism or generally as a realist view of science or even as post-positivism (Fraser et al 1991, Phillips 1990). It is based on the work of Michael Scriven, Roy Bhaskar, and notably, the philosopher Rom Harre. This epistemological model seeks to incorporate the critiques of logical positivism without abandoning the concept of a knowable reality, as its basis is in realism. The realist theory of science 'allows scientists to believe that they are grappling with entities that, although often not observable directly, are real enough...It would seem that once they understand it, scientists would happily adopt a realist theory of science' (Manicas and Secord, 1983, p. 412).

The ontology of scientific realism is critical realist. Reality exists external to the observer, and although it cannot be apprehended as it is (for the observer's theoretical orientation acts as a filter), one can strive for an approximation of this reality. As scientific knowledge develops, what appears to be an approximation of reality today may not be so tomorrow (hence the term 'fallibilistic'). In this sense, scientific realism shares the same critical realism as most of empirical practice, pragmatism, and critical theory perspectives in social work research. However, it goes further than all of these others, in recognising that the world is an open system which consists of a constellation of structures, mechanisms and contexts.

According to Bhaskar (1978, p. 24), scientific realism:

regards the objects of knowledge as the structures and mechanisms that generate phenomena; and the knowledge is produced in the social activities of science. These objects are neither phenomena (empiricism) nor human constructs imposed upon the phenomena (idealism) but real structures which endure independently of our knowledge, our experience, and the conditions which allow us access to them.

Phenomena that are studied in the real world are studied in a fluid context, that is, in an open system. The activities of persons in society may be seen as a set of interacting, interwoven structures at different levels. Realism refers to the embeddedness of all human action within a wider range of social processes as the 'stratified nature of social reality. Even the most mundane actions make sense only because they contain in-built assumptions about a wider set of social rules and institutions' (Pawson and Tilley, 1997a, p. 406). Establishing the existence and properties of these things, and the construction of confirmable explanatory theories about structure and their properties, are the products of both theoretical and experimental work. Different disciplines and different investigators may organise their apprehension of phenomena differently; however, the perspectives that guide any scientific study must be made explicit.

Rather than concentrate on events and the linking of variables at the surface (e.g. the mere establishment of cause and effect relationships between the intervention and its effects), scientific realism addresses the questions of why a programme works, for whom, and in what circumstances---the perspective is holistic. Although a researcher may not be able to achieve such a holistic picture of social work practice, with such a perspective one may be more aware of limitations of the research that is attempted, and also more aware of its exact contribution to the whole, and what needs to be addressed in the future. As in pragmatism, a multi-method approach is used---scientific realism is wholeheartedly methodological-pluralist; but unlike pragmatism the evaluator does not only respond to the needs of practice in order to judge it, but also retains a holistic approach to reality, in order to improve practice.

As a perspective of research into practice, scientific realism can address four key questions for practitioners: how to select a model of intervention, how to use effectiveness research in the selection process, how to target the intervention in pre-existing contexts, and how to improve the intervention models based on evaluation research.

Scientific realism is based on a scientific approach to the construction of models of intervention. Unlike empirical practice that has no account of the content of theories to be tested, the realist scientific schema has a rational process for the invention of theories, as described by the philosopher Harre (1984, p. 57-8):

there are ideal forms of reasoning at work in that area of human thinking too. They have to do with the canons of constructing and imagining models, and thus depends upon principles governing the rational way to make comparisons, to judge likenesses against unlikenesses. They lead to areas of structure more complex than the deductive relationships that are to be found at work in the organised parts of mathematics.

Scientific researchers build models in an attempt to apprehend the realities, and on the basis of comparisons as approximations of reality, improve the model-building in a dialectic relationship between the construction of the model and its analogous comparisons with reality. In social work, practitioners construct models in their practice, which includes their theoretical orientation, practice wisdom, accepted knowledge amongst peers, tacit knowledge, and previous experience of what works, for whom and in what contexts. Starting with the existing model of practice (Figure 7.2), the practitioner makes an assessment (in partnership with the client) which leads to hypotheses about what might work, for whom, and in what contexts. Then through observation and other multi-method data gathering of information regarding the pre-existing mechanisms, contexts and outcomes, the practitioner is able to make the intervention programme more specific and to aim it in such a way that it harnesses enabling mechanisms and steers clear of disabling mechanisms. At this stage, the multi-method data-gathering addresses the questions of what actually works, for whom and in what contexts. And all this feeds back into the theory that we started from, in a realist effectiveness cycle.

In this way, evaluation research is about improving the construction of models, and therefore about improving the content of the practice itself. Evidence is used to better target and better adjust the content of the programme in such a way that it can have a generative impact on pre-existing mechanisms and contexts to help bring about the desired changes. The evidence from data collection methods such as single-case evaluation can be used to prove the programme's effectiveness and to make judgements about its effectiveness, but this is a by-product. The main purpose of this evidence-gathering is to improve the model. Objectivity lies not just in the use of measures, but in the extent to which the model is analogous with reality. At each cycle, a better approximation of reality is obtained, as compared with the previous cycle. In this way, scientific realism addresses all the dimensions and questions of effectiveness of practice which others cannot--including content, outcomes, the perceptions of all involved, ethics and values, and contexts.

The rules of scientific realism include the addressing of the following: how and why a programme has the potential to cause change, how it informs and alters choices that people make, how problem causal mechanisms are countered by the programme's alternative causal mechanisms, how problem mechanisms are activated in contexts, how a generative mechanism (i.e. the programme of intervention) can be fired successfully, what are outcomes and how they are produced. Realism addresses the real structures or context-mechanism-outcome configurations, and the questions of what works, for whom, and in what circumstances, to improve future practice or the construction of future models of good practice.

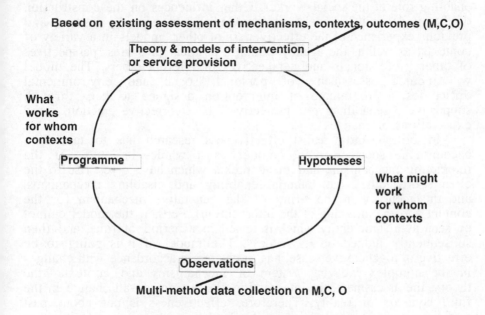

Figure 7.2   The realist effectiveness cycle
Adapted from Pawson and Tilley (1997)

Contribution of Scientific Realism

The other main paradigms in contemporary British social work practice research---empirical practice, pragmatism and critical theory---offer their own contributions to the theory and practice of effectiveness research, but as a world view there are limitations in each of these approaches, and they tend to emphasise one or the other parts of the real entities in which social work operates. Therefore they fail to address the complexities of social work in a holistic way, and their main purpose tends to be making judgements of past practice with the hope of influencing future practice. The scientific realist approach, on the other hand, encourages the inquirer to seek a wider view of effectiveness in an attempt to apprehend the complex reality of social work practice as it is. Based on the construction and testing of models of practice, this approach not only enables judgements to be made about past practice, but is also inextricably linked to improving future practice.

The social worker constructs a model that attempts to explain reality, and based on this explanation, aims to change reality. Depending upon the ethics and values underpinning practice, this model may be constructed in partnership with the service user, in keeping with the enabling role of the social worker. Other influences on the construction of the model will include tacit knowledge and practice wisdom, and previous experience of the effectiveness of other models in a variety of contexts; as well as the agency policies, political pressures, perspectives of other professionals and perspectives of relevant others. The model will include assessments of personal, social and environmental difficulties, a programme of intervention designed to help through supportive, rehabilitative, protective or corrective action, and expectations of changes.

In other words, realist effectiveness research has to take into account the social worker's model as a whole---its study of the interacting mechanisms and the contexts which have given rise to the client's difficulties, the potential enabling and disabling mechanisms, and the accuracy in the firing of the generative mechanism (or the content and the targeting of the intervention). Further, the model cannot be seen as a static entity which is tested in a period of time, and then subsequently judged on its success. The model, if it is going to be effective in a generative sense, has to change in accordance with changes in the complex weaving system of mechanisms and contexts---the theory, the assessment, the intervention, the outcomes---all change in the fluid contexts of reality. Therefore, effectiveness is not about past performance---a central purpose of effectiveness research is to improve this model-building process. Evidence is collected in a methodological-pluralist approach in which the multiple perspectives are studied at a minimum, using a variety of data gathering techniques. This evidence may provide information about the effectiveness of the model---its accuracy, its impact on other mechanisms, its impact on contexts---but this is a by-product.

The central purpose of this evidence is to improve the programme both in terms of its content and targeting, to improve the theory, and to improve the assessment, and thereby to improve the mix of data gathering techniques, in a continuous cycle of improvement. In realist effectiveness research, the objectivity of the evidence lies not in the type of measures used, but in the way the model as a whole is analogous to the realities of the open system---and the continuous feedback from effectiveness research enables a dialectical relationship between the process of model-building and the reality that it seeks to apprehend.

An important contribution of scientific realism is that it is inclusive of all the other realist perspectives including empirical practice, pragmatism and critical theory. The scientific realist perspective in social work practice research is a new perspective that is being applied and tested at the present time. There are, as yet, no published examples, and therefore as far as its limitations are concerned, the jury is still out. However, the inclusive nature of this perspective provides new and exciting possibilities for the use of methodologies such as single-case evaluation within a perspective that is based not only on methodological pluralism, but also retains a holistic approach to evaluating professional practice. Within this perspective, single-case evaluation can contribute to providing data regarding client progress, and at the same time other forms of data-gathering would provide further evidence to build up knowledge regarding what works for whom and in what contexts.

Example of single-case evaluation within a scientific realist perspective

At the time of writing, a second project is underway, this time with trained probation officers, to pilot the use of single-case designs in probation work with adult offenders. Three of the practice teachers who took part in the earlier project and are themselves acting as consultants in this new project, raised some limitations and questions from their experience of the study (Chapter 4) in a workshop organised for the participating probation officers in which the author was asked to introduce single-case evaluation. Having had the time to reflect on their experience of the first project, the three practice teachers were very positive about the way single-case evaluation had been used and the evidence of effectiveness that the project had generated. However, they also identified a number of limitations and questions that had arisen from the way the methodology had been used earlier. These limitations and questions arose from the practice teachers' own reflections.

Before dealing with these issues, the author provided examples of the use of the methodology, and explained its basic requirements, and what it was able to do, and what it could not do, as in the previous project. However, this time, the methodology was presented as part of a realist framework of effectiveness. This was very well received, and appeared to iron out the main limitations and questions raised from the first project. The starting point was the practitioner's existing theoretical model which also formed the basis of an assessment of the mechanisms, contexts and objectives (or expected outcomes, e.g. effects concerning offending and the mechanisms and contexts in which such behaviour was embedded). This process was not purely theoretical, but it applied a theoretical framework to the process of assessment based on the evidence so far, which led into the hypotheses---what might work with this client, and what were the contexts that impinge on the offending behaviour and other identified mechanisms.

The cyclical process then continued into the use of data-gathering techniques, and single-case designs were presented as one possible means of fulfilling this, along with other appropriate methodologies. This provided data on the mechanisms, contexts and outcomes that were identified earlier in the cycle--and the connection of the practitioner's model to the real needs and circumstances of the client. This evidence then led to the specificity and targeting of the programme of intervention, seen as a generative mechanism to effect change in the identified mechanisms and contexts that impinged on the client and his/her situation. This process then fed back into the theory and assessment, to further develop the theory and the assessment as a model that explained and impacted upon the client's reality. Having discussed this effectiveness cycle in some depth, it was possible to clarify the limitations and questions that had arisen from the first project, as in the foregoing. The questions raised by the practice teachers are presented as quotes.

Distinction between intervention and the measures used

Q.1. Although efforts were made to make a distinction between the intervention programme and the instruments used to measure its effects upon the client, sometimes the process of measurement itself became part of the intervention. This was seen as a problem, as the stated purpose of the use of single-case designs was to test the hypotheses that the intervention programmes would lead to the desired effects.

The distinction between the intervention and the measures used to test its effects is a heuristic device, and sometimes this distinction can be blurred. This distinction becomes crucial in the empirical practice approach, as the outcome measures are used to test the hypotheses that the intervention would lead to certain desired effects. However, all such activities are theory-laden and not theory-neutral. Therefore, as the theoretical framework that influences the practitioner's assessment and choice of intervention, also influences the choice of outcome indicators, there is bound to be a blurring of the distinction between the intervention and the selected demonstrable referents. Further, in practice, a meaningful use of some measures---e.g. rating scales---requires anchoring of its points in terms of the client's circumstances and the client's definitions of what is worse and what is better, and therefore such a discussion may itself be part of an intervention---for example, as part of a cognitive process.

However, in a realist effectiveness framework, this distinction between the intervention and its effects no longer has the same importance as in the previous empirical practice approach. That is because the use of single-case designs itself becomes part of the process to develop the practitioner's model on which the intervention is based. The systematic tracking of client progress is also aimed at improving the programme itself as well as the assessment and theoretical framework of the practitioner. The main purpose is no longer to simply provide evidence of effectiveness to demonstrate that the intervention had worked---it is to help effect developments in the process of intervention itself. Therefore, the distinction between the intervention and the process of measurement of its effects is no longer an important issue. At the same time, the systematic tracking of client progress can be used as evidence of effectiveness---but that is only a by-product. In a realist study, it is the development of the model itself that is of primary concern.

Content of interventions

Q.2. The emphasis had been on the use of measures and the methodology, almost to the exclusion of the content of the intervention, which was not really part of the methodology's remit. The tendency had been to see the intervention as a static entity, and the purpose of the methodology was almost exclusively the measuring of effects.

This is a perennial problem in empirical practice research---there is a tendency to ignore content, and to see the intervention as a static entity that is being tested with the measures of effectiveness, and the focus of research becomes the measures themselves. However, in a realist perspective, the theory and content are central, and therefore, the purpose for the use of single-case evaluation and other methodologies would be to help in the development of the model---the development of the theory, assessment, intervention programme---and effecting changes through the generative mechanism in the contexts of the client. In this way, the process is no longer methodological-driven, but the methodology serves the central purpose of explanation of reality in order to make the intervention more effective in the client's circumstances. Within the realist perspective, the explanations sought are not just what works for adult offenders, but what kinds of interventions work best for what kinds of probation clients, under what conditions, and in what particular contexts. The systematic tracking of client progress through single-case evaluation provides data along with other methodologies to inform this process of developing the intervention programmes.

The selection of measures

Q.3. A tendency was to go straight into quantitative measures, i.e., to concentrate on providing systematic measurement of only those problems that could be measured in this way. This raised a supplementary question-- how is the selection of measures arrived at, and how soon?

As the philosopher Rom Harre explains, the scientific process involves the use of models as plausible connections to reality, or as likeness to reality which can improve the explanation of reality, which help to make the intervention effective within the contexts and structures and other mechanisms that are the real entities of which the client is an integral part. When scientists lose confidence in their ability to construct such models, they lapse into a concentration on effects. Rather than develop your theoretical framework and assessment of the realities, at a time when you are under pressure to demonstrate your effectiveness to the Home Office and others, you return from depth to the surface (i.e. outcomes at the surface of the box in Figure 7.1). You no longer concentrate on the real entities or processes that explain real entities. Rather, you take the easy way out, and say, here you are---see I am effective, the results are positive. This is simpler to do, because you are at the surface, you are making a link between your intervention and the effects, but you do not have to explain why, or effect meaningful changes in your client's circumstances, or focus on the development of your theoretical model, or on attempts to turn your models into explanatory structures that tell the real stories about the clients realities and how they can be changed.

As for the supplementary question, it is related to the first. Take the 'SMART' initiative within your agency (an acronym for a movement that emphasises the formulation of objectives for probation supervision of offenders--the objectives should be Specific, Measurable, Agreed, Realistic, Time-limited). It should be commended for establishing a focus on realistic objectives, but to suggest that they should be measurable implies that you should not have objectives that are not measurable at any time. In a realist approach, there are three types of problems, as explained by Harre's referential realism. First, there are the problems that are immediately obvious---for example, you could immediately measure the client's attendance as part of the reporting requirements of the probation order. That is a problem with an immediate, demonstrable referent. Second, there are problems that are likely to exist, based on your theoretical framework, hypotheses and the assessment that you have made with the client; but at the present time, you can only get some indicators of existence, for example indirect measures, or some rating scales which provide an indication of existence. You can begin measuring these too, although there would be greater imperfections in the data. Third, there are problems that you think probably exist, based on your theoretical framework, practice wisdom, and prevailing opinions, but no empirical referents are possible at this stage. You will not measure these until some indicators can become available, but they are not ignored---on the contrary, they are part of your model. These are the three types of problems you would be dealing with, in a realist paradigm. Have confidence in your models, and avoid the tendency to run back from depth to the surface.

Fears amongst practitioners

> Q.4. A minority of practitioners had been suspicious of the project---they had said, for example, 'This is de-skilling me. I know that my approach to practice works, why do I need to express it on paper in the form of graphs? Is the sole purpose to provide evidence of effectiveness, and if so, for whom? Is it part of the movement to use cognitive-behavioural approach on the grounds that it works better?

Shaw (1996) and Everitt and Hardiker (1996) are also suspicious of evaluation that is imposed by management. They arrive at this from the perspective of critical theory, and their aims are to protect the professions from such impositions, and to wrest effectiveness research back from management and use it to emancipate both service users and practitioners. There are merits in such a suspicion. What is really happening is that the managers are responding to the pressures from government and society to demonstrate effectiveness, at a time when, as Parton (1994a) explains, truths about the foundations of social work and the welfare state are no longer taken for granted, and social work is being deconstructed from what it was, and is being reconstructed in different ways. These managers have lost confidence in your models of service delivery and are concentrating on demonstrating effectiveness. What you, as practitioners, need to do is not only demonstrate effectiveness (as a by-product), but use data gathering techniques as part of the cycle to develop your models of practice. When you see the process from a realist perspective, you do not have to feel de-skilled.

Have confidence in your existing models, and use effectiveness research to develop them. In this way, you can integrate single-case designs and/or other methods to provide evidence that your model works (if that is your finding), and develop it so that the model works even better in the future. The evidence of practice from data-gathering methods will inform the development of your programme, your theoretical framework, your assessment, and your hypotheses. What single-case evaluation could add to your process of gathering evidence is consistency in the sense of systematic data on the mechanisms, contexts and outcomes. In this way, the effectiveness research will help to develop your practice further, even if you are already confident with your existing models---and you could also develop newer, improved models, based on your experience of previous models.

Macdonald (1996) and others rightly say that your selection of intervention methods should be based on the evidence of effectiveness. The question is, what does 'evidence' mean? If the evidence is based on outcome data alone, without proper consideration of the content of social work practice as well as the contexts of practice, then this evidence is not sufficient as there would be no explanation of why an intervention was successful with some clients and not successful with others. On the other hand, if the evidence is obtained through the same and/or other data gathering methods from a realist perspective, as outlined in Figure 7.2, then the effectiveness research process has greater explanatory powers to enable such selections to be made. A realist approach enables you to base your existing models on evidence which becomes part of the process of development of such models in addressing the mechanisms and contexts of your practice. It also enables you to discover new models of interventions on the basis of what works, for whom and in what circumstances. In a realist framework, you will be continuously developing existing models and/or searching for new models that can be applied to the real entities that your practice addresses.

The above four limitations and questions arising from the first project (Chapter 4), and the answers as above, also indicate that what is decisive is not any methodology in itself, but the paradigmatic framework of the inquirer. The same methodology (in this case single-case evaluation) is not only applied differently, but the inquirer's effectiveness questions are also different, from a realist perspective. Rather than provide descriptions at the surface of Figure 7.1, the methodology (or a mix of methodologies) becomes part of an enterprise searching for explanations in greater depth, in helping to provide evidence which forms part of the process of the construction of models to address the mechanisms and contexts of adult offenders. A further issue here is that single-case designs alone are unable to provide the data that would be required in a realist framework (e.g. the multiple perspectives), and therefore the realist inquirer does not depend on one method alone, but is whole-heartedly pluralist in the selection of methods that address the questions that emerge from the real entities of social work effectiveness.

Empirical practice as a 'black box' foundation

Each of the perspectives included here (empirical practice, pragmatism, critical theory and scientific realism) has an important role to play in addressing the complexities of practice, and each sets out to achieve this goal in its own way. Adapting Michael Scriven's terminology of 'black', 'grey' and 'white box' evaluations (Scriven 1994), 'black box' evaluation is where the researcher concentrates on evaluating a programme's effects, without addressing the components that make up the programme. Such research is crucially important, and stands in its own right---this is the role of much empirical practice research. Studies which use single-case evaluation alone will fall into this category--the concentration is on effects, and the content of interventions is not analysed---hence the black box with its contents well-hidden.

The 'grey box' evaluation is where the components of a programme are discerned, but their inner workings or principles of operation are not fully revealed---this is the contribution of much pragmatic and critical theorist research. For this purpose, single-case evaluation will not be able to provide all the answers---other methods will have to be used to address the wider questions.

Scientific realism attempts a 'white box' evaluation, which not only addresses the effects, but also the inner workings and operations of the components of a programme and how they are connected. Such a perspective has a great deal of promise for evidence-based approaches and methodologies such as single-case evaluation. Each methodology will be seen for what it can or cannot do, and an appropriate mix will be applied to address all of the evaluation questions. The perspective will be holistic, and seek to critically analyse the utility of any study involving the evaluation of practice, from the perspective of what it contributes to the dimensions of practice as in Figure 7.1, and what else needs to be done to address the full complexities of practice.

When the purposes of evaluation are categorised within these three types of boxes, it is important to recognise that empirical practice which concentrates on the evaluation of effects (e.g. through single-case evaluation or group designs) forms the basis in each type of box. Other methods are added to address the wider questions, but it is assumed that empirical practice as in the form of the 'black box' remains. In this sense, the other perspectives add blocks to this process. To throw out empirical practice for critical theory (as Shaw 1998 attempts to do) is like throwing out the baby with the bath water. It is important to recognise what each perspective contributes to the needs of practice evaluation as illustrated in Figure 7.1, and to adopt an inclusive approach where one perspective does not have to destroy another in order to create a niche for itself.

Bibliography

Allen, I., Hogg, D. and Peace, S. (1992), *Elderly People: Choice, Participation and Satisfaction,* Policy Studies Institute, London.

Alter, C. and Evens, W. (1990), *Evaluating Your Practice*, Springer, New York.

Anastas, J.W. and MacDonald, M.L. (1994), *Research Design for Social Work and the Human Services*, Lexington Books, New York.

Audit Commission (1992), *The Community Revolution: Personal Services and Community Care*, HMSO, London.

Barlow, D.H., Hayes, S.C. and Nelsen, R.O. (1984), *The Scientist Practitioner*, Pergamon, New York.

Barlow, D.H. and Hersen, M. (1984), *Single Case Experimental Designs: Strategies for Studying Behaviour Change*, 2nd. edition, Pergamon Press, New York.

Bentley, K.J. (1990), 'An Evaluation of Family-Based Intervention With Schizophrenia Using Single-System Research', *British Journal of Social Work,* vol. 20, pp. 101-116.

Bhaskar, R. (1978), *A Realist Theory of Science*, 2nd. edition, Harvester, Brighton.

Bloom, M. and Fischer, J. (1982), *Evaluating Practice: Guidelines for The Accountable Professional*, Prentice-Hall Inc., Englewood Cliffs, N.J.

Bloom, M., Fischer, J. and Orme, J. (1995), *Evaluating Practice: Guidelines for The Accountable Professional*, 2nd. edition, Allyn and Bacon, Boston.

Blyth, E., Kazi, M.A.F. and Milner, J. (1994), 'Education Reform and Education Social Work in Britain', *Social Work in Education,* vol. 16, pp. 129-134.

Blythe, B.J. (1995), 'Single-System Design', in Edwards, R.L. et al. (eds) *Encyclopaedia of Social Work*, 19th. edition, vol. 3, National Association of Social Workers, Silver Spring, Maryland, pp. 2164-2168.

Blythe, B. J. and Rodgers, A.Y. (1993), 'Evaluating Our Own Practice: Past, Present, and Future Trends', co-published in *Journal of Social Service Review* vol. 18(1/2), pp. 101-119, and in Bloom, M. (ed) *Single-System Designs in the Social Services: Issues and Options for the 1990s*, Haworth, Binghampton, N.Y., pp. 101-119.

Blythe, B.J. and Tripodi, T. (1989), *Measurement in Direct Practice*, Sage Publications, Newbury Park, Ca..

Bostwick, G.J. Jr. and Kyte, N.S. (1993), 'Measurement in Research', in Grinnell, R.M. Jr. (ed) *Social Work Research And Evaluation*, Fourth edition, F.E. Peacock, Itasca, Ill, pp. 174-197.

Brennan, J. (ed) (1992), *Mixing Methods: Qualitative and Quantitative Research*, Avebury, Aldershot.

Bryman, A. (1988). *Quantity and Quality in Social Research*, Unwin Hyman, London.

Campbell, D.T. and Stanley, J.C. (1963), *Experimental and Quasi-Experimental Designs for Research*, Rand Mcnally, Chicago.

CCETSW (1989), *Requirements and Regulations for the Diploma in Social Work*, Paper no. 30, Central Council for Education and Training in Social Work, London.

Cheetham, J. (1998), 'The Evaluation of Social Work: Priorities, Problems and Possibilities', in Cheetham, J. and Kazi, M. A. F. (eds) *The Working of Social Work*, Jessica Kingsley, London, pp. 9-29.

Cheetham, J., Fuller, R., Mcivor, G. and Petch, A. (1992), *Evaluating Social Work Effectiveness*, Open University Press, Buckingham.

Corcoran, K. and Fischer, J. (1987), *Measures for Clinical Practice: A Source Book*, The Free Press, New York.

England, H. (1986), *Social Work as an Art*, Allen and Unwin, London.

Everitt, A. and Hardiker, P. (1996), *Evaluating for Good Practice*, Macmillan, Basingstoke.

Fischer, J. (1981), 'The Social Work Revolution', *Social Work*, vol. 26, pp. 199-207.

Fischer, J. and Corcoran, K. (1994), *Measures for Clinical Practice: A Source Book*, vols. 1 and 2, The Free Press, New York.

Fraser, M., Taylor, M.J., Jackson, R. and O'jack, J. (1991), 'Social Work and Science: Many Ways of Knowing?', *Social Work Research and Abstracts*, vol. 27, pp. 5-15.

Fuller, R. (1996), 'Evaluating Social Work Effectiveness: a Pragmatic Approach', in Alderson, P., Brill, S., Chalmers, I., Fuller, R., Hinkley-Smith, P., Macdonald, G., Newman, T., Oakley, A., Roberts, H. and Ward, H. (eds) *What Works? Effective Social Interventions in Child Welfare*, Barnardos, Ilford, Essex, pp. 55-67.

Fuller, R. and Petch, A. (1995) *Practitioner Research: The Reflexive Social Worker*, Open University Press, Buckingham.

Gambrill, E. D. and Barth, R. P. (1980), 'Single-Case Study Designs Revisited', *Social Work Research and Abstracts*, vol. 16, pp. 15-20.

Gingerich, W.J. (1984), 'Methodological Observations on Applied Behavioural Science', *Journal of Applied Behaviour Science*, vol. 20, pp. 71-79.

Guba, E. C. (1990), 'The Alternative Paradigm Dialogue' in Guba, E.G. (ed) *The Paradigm Dialogue*, Sage Publications, Thousand Oaks, pp. 17-27.

Harre, R. (1984), *The Philosophies of Science: An Introductory Survey*, 2nd. edition, Oxford University Press, Oxford.

Harris, R. (1996), 'Telling Tales: Probation in the Contemporary Social Formation', in Parton, N. (ed) *Social Theory, Social Change and Social Work*, Routledge, London, pp. 115-134.

Hayles, M. and Kazi, M.A.F. (1998), 'Making a Difference: The Impact of a Single-Case Evaluation Project', *Probation Journal*, vol. 45, pp. 27-32.

Hersen, M. and Barlow, D.H. (1976), *Single Case Experimental Designs: Strategies for Studying Behaviour Change*, First edition, Pergamon Press, New York.

Hudson, W.W. (1982), *The Clinical Measurement Package: A Field Manual*, Dorsey Press, Chicago, Ill.

Jayaratne, S. and Levy, R.L. (1979), *Empirical Clinical Practice*, Columbia University Press, New York.

Jeffery, D.R. and Good, D.C. (1995), 'Rehabilitation of the Stroke Patient', *Current Opinion in Neurology*, vol. 8, pp. 62-68.

Johansson, B.B. (1995), 'Has Sensory Stimulation a Role in Stroke Rehabilitation?' in *Scandinavian Journal of Rehabilitation Medicine*, vol. 29, pp. 87-96.

Jordan, B. (1978), "A Comment on 'Theory and Practice in Social Work'", *British Journal of Social Work*, vol. 8, pp. 23-25.

Kazdin, A.E. (1982), *Single-Case Research Designs*, Oxford University Press, New York.

Kazdin, A.E. (1984), 'Statistical Analyses for Single-Case Experimental Designs', in Barlow, D.H. and Hersen, M., *Single Case Experimental Designs: Strategies for Studying Behaviour Change*, Pergamon Press, New York, pp. 285-324.

Kazi, M.A.F. (1996), 'The Centre for Evaluation Studies at the University of Huddersfield: A Profile', *Research on Social Work Practice*, vol. 6, pp. 104-116.

Kazi, M.A.F. (1996a), 'Single-Case Evaluation in the Public Sector', *Evaluation*, vol. 2, pp. 85-97.

Kazi, M. A. F. (1997), 'Single-Case Evaluation in British Social Services' in Chelimsky, E., and Shadish, W. R. (eds) *Evaluation for the 21st Century: A Resource Book*, Sage Publications, Thousand Oaks, pp. 419-442.

Kazi, M.A.F. (1997a), *Towards a Pragmatic Approach to the Proper Method Mix*, Paper presented at the 1997 European Evaluation Society Conference 'Evaluation: What Works and for Whom?', Stockholm, March 6-8, 1997.

Kazi, M. A. F. (1998), 'Putting Single-Case Evaluation into Practice', in Cheetham, J. and Kazi, M. A. F. (eds) *The Working of Social Work*, Jessica Kingsley, London, pp. 187-199.

Kazi, M. A. F. (1998a), *Practice Research in England,* invited paper presented at the International Conference 'Research for Social Work Practice', Florida International University, Miami, January 24-26, 1998.

Kazi, M.A.F., Craven, M. and Wilson, J. (1995), *Evaluation of the Kirklees Gest 20 Programme: Truancy and Disaffection*, The Centre for Evaluation Studies, University of Huddersfield, Huddersfield, England.

Kazi, M.A.F. and Firth, K., (1997), *Evaluation of Oakes villa Rehabilitation Unit*, The Centre for Evaluation Studies, University of Huddersfield, Huddersfield, England.

Kazi, M.A.F. and Hayles, M. (1996), *Single-Case Evaluation in a Probation Service*, The Centre for Evaluation Studies, University of Huddersfield, Huddersfield, England.

Kazi, M.A.F., Mantysaari, M. and Rostila, I. (1997), 'Promoting the Use of Single-Case Designs: Social Work Experiences from England and Finland', *Research on Social Work Practice*, vol. 7, pp. 311-328.

Kazi, M.A.F. and Wilson, J. (1993), *Applying Outcome Measures in Direct Client Services*, The Centre for Evaluation Studies, University of Huddersfield, Huddersfield, England.

Kazi, M.A.F. and Wilson, J. (1996), 'Applying Single-Case Evaluation in Social Work', *British Journal of Social Work*, vol. 26. pp. 699-717.

Kazi, M.A.F. and Wilson, J. (1996a), 'Applying Single-Case Evaluation Methodology in a British Social Work Agency', *Research on Social Work Practice'*, vol. 6, pp. 5-26.

Kratochwill, T.R. (1978), 'Foundations of Time-Series Research', in Kratochwill, T.R. (ed) *Single Subject Research: Strategies for Evaluating Change*, Academic Press, Orlando, Fl.

Krishef, C.H. (1991), *Fundamental Approaches to Single Subject Design and Analysis*, Krieger Publishing Company, Malabar, Fl.

McGuire, J. and Priestley, P. (1995), "Reviewing 'What Works': Past, Present and Future", in McGuire, J. (ed) *What Works: Reducing Reoffending,* Wiley, Chichester, pp. 3-34.

Macdonald, G. (1994), 'Developing Empirically-Based Practice in Probation', *British Journal of Social Work*, vol. 24, pp. 405-427.

Macdonald, G. (1996), 'Ice Therapy: Why We Need Randomised Controlled Trials', in Alderson, P., Brill, S., Chalmers, I., Fuller, R., Hinkley-Smith, P., Macdonald, G., Newman, T., Oakley, A., Roberts, H. and Ward, H. (eds) *What Works? Effective Social Interventions in Child Welfare*, Barnardos, Ilford, Essex, pp. 16-32.

Manicas, P. T. (1987), *A History and Philosophy of the Social Sciences*, Oxford: Basil Blackwell.

Manicas, P.T. and Secord, P.F. (1983), 'Implications for Psychology of the New Philosophy of Science', *American Psychologist*, vol. 38, pp. 399-413.

Marsh, P. and Fisher, M, (1992), *Good Intentions: Developing Partnership in Social Services*, Joseph Rowntree Foundation, York.

Marshall, K., Weaver, P., and Loewenstein, P. (1991), *Targets for Change,* Nottinghamshire Probation Service, Nottingham.

Martin, L.L. and Kettner, P.M. (1996), *Measuring the Performance of Human Service Programs*, Sage Publications, Thousand Oaks.

Medawar, P. (1982), *Pluto's Republic*, Oxford University Press, Oxford.

Mutschler, E. (1984), 'Evaluating Practice: A Study of Research Utilisation by Practitioners', *Social Work*, vol. 29, pp. 332-337.

Nelsen, J.C. (1988), 'Single-Subject Research', in Grinnell, R.M. jr. (ed), *Social Work Research and Evaluation*, Third edition, F.E. Peacock, Itasca, Ill., pp. 362-399.

Oakley, A. (1996), 'Who's Afraid of the Randomised Controlled Trial? The Challenge of Evaluating the Potential of Social Interventions', in Alderson, P., Brill, S., Chalmers, I., Fuller, R., Hinkley-Smith, P., Macdonald, G., Newman, T., Oakley, A., Roberts, H. and Ward, H. (eds) *What Works? Effective Social Interventions in Child Welfare*, Barnardos, Ilford, Essex, pp. 33-47.

Outhwaite, W. (1987), *New Philosophies of Social Science: Realism, Hermeneutics and Critical Theory*, Macmillan, London.

Parton, N. (1994), 'The Nature of Social Work Under Conditions of (Post) Modernity', *Social Work and Social Sciences Review,* vol. 5, pp. 93-112.

Parton, N. (1994a), '"Problematics of Government', (Post) Modernity and Social Work"', *British Journal of Social Work*, vol. 24, pp. 9-32.

Pawson, R. and Tilley, N. (1997a), 'An Introduction to Scientific Realist Evaluation', in Chelimsky, E., and Shadish, W. R. (eds) *Evaluation for the 21st Century: A Resource Book*, Sage Publications, Thousand Oaks, pp. 405-418.

Pawson, R. and Tilley, N. (1997), *Realistic Evaluation*, Sage Publications, Thousand Oaks.

Penka, E.P. and Kirk, S.A. (1991), 'Practitioner Involvement in Clinical Evaluation', *Social Work*, vol. 36, pp. 513-518.

Phillips, C.J., Palfrey, C.F., Harding, H.N., Pickard, S. and Urquhart, R.J. (1993), 'Monitoring and Evaluation of Selected Projects Under the Initiative for the Care of the Elderly in Wales,' in Robbins, D. (ed) *Community Care: Findings From Department of Health Funded Research 1988-1992*, HMSO, London.

Phillips, D. C. (1990), 'Postpositivistic Science: Myths and Realities', in Guba, E.G. (ed) *The Paradigm Dialogue*, Sage Publications, Thousand Oaks, pp. 31-45.

Polster, R.A. and Collins, D. (1993), 'Structured Observation', in Grinnell Jr., R.M. (ed) *Social Work Research and Evaluation*, Fourth edition, Itasca, Ill.: F.E. Peacock, pp. 244-261.

Popkewitz, T. S. (1990), 'Whose Future? Whose Past? Notes on Critical Theory and Methodology', in Guba, E.G. (ed) *The Paradigm Dialogue*, Sage Publications, Thousand Oaks, pp. 46-66.

Rees, S. and Wallace, A. (1982), *Verdicts on Social Work*, Edward Arnold, London.

Riddoch, M.J., Humphreys, G.W. and Bateman, A. (1995), 'Stroke: Issues in Recovery and Rehabilitation', *Physiotherapy*, vol. 81, pp. 689-694.

Roberts, C. (1991), 'What works - Using Social Work Methods to Reduce Re-offending in Serious and Persistent Offenders', in *Proceedings of the ACOP Annual Conference, University of York 1991*, Association of Chief Probation Officers, Wakefield, England.

Robinson, E.A.R., Bronson, D.E., and Blythe, B.J. (1988), 'An Analysis of the Implementation of Single-Case Evaluation by Practitioners', *Social Service Review*, vol. 62, pp. 285-301.

Robson, C. (1993), *Real World Research*, Blackwell, Oxford.

Scriven, M. (1994), 'The fine line between evaluation and explanation', *Evaluation Practice*, vol. 15, pp. 75-77.

Shaw, I. (1996), *Evaluating in Practice,* Arena, Aldershot.

Shaw, I. (1998), 'Practising evaluation', in Cheetham, J. and Kazi, M. A. F. (eds) *The Working of Social Work*, Jessica Kingsley, London, pp. 201-223.

Sheldon, B. (1978), 'Theory and practice in social work: A rexamination of a tenuous relationship', *British Journal of Social Work*, vol. 8, pp. 1-22.

Sheldon, B. (1982a), 'A Measure of Success', *Social Work Today*, vol. 13, pp. 8-11.

Sheldon, B. (1982b), *Behaviour Modification*, Tavistock Publications, London.

Sheldon, B. (1983), 'The Use of Single Case Experimental Designs in the Evaluation of Social Work', *British Journal of Social Work,* vol. 13, pp. 477-500.

Sheldon, B. (1984), 'Single Case Evaluation Methods', in Lishman, J. (ed) *Evaluation*, Jessica Kingsley, London, pp. 47-67.

Sheldon, B. (1984a), 'Evaluation With One Eye Closed: The Empiricist Agenda in Social Work Research---A Reply To Peter Raynor', *British Journal of Social Work*, vol. 14, pp. 635-637.

Sheldon, B. (1986), 'Social Work Effectiveness Experiments: Review and Implications', *British Journal of Social Work,* vol. 16, pp. 233-42.

Sheldon, B. (1987), 'Implementing Findings From Social Work Effectiveness Research', in *British Journal of Social Work*, vol. 17, pp. 573-586.

Sheldon, B. (1988), 'Single Case Evaluation Methods: Review and Prospects', in Lishman, J. (ed) *Evaluation*, 2nd. edition, Jessica Kingsley, London, pp. 40-57.

Shemmings, D. and Shemmings, Y. (1995), 'Defining Participative Practice in Health and Welfare' in Jack, R. (ed) *Empowerment in Community Care*, Chapman and Hall, London, pp. 43-58.

Skinner, B.F. (1974), *About Behaviourism*, Cape, London.

Tawney, J.W. and Gast, D.L. (1984), *Single Subject Research in Special Education*, Macmillan, New York.

Thyer, B.A. (1993), 'Single-System Research Designs' in Grinnell, R.M. jr. (ed) *Social Work Research and Evaluation*, fourth edition, F.E. Peacock, Itasca, Ill., pp. 94-117.

Thyer, B.A. (1993a), 'Social Work Theory and Practice Research: The Approach of Logical Positivism', *Social Work and Social Sciences Review*, vol. 4, pp. 5-26.

Thyer, B.A. and Wodarski, J.S. (1998), 'First Principles of Empirical Social Work Practice' in Thyer, B.A. and Wodarski, J.S. (eds) *Handbook of Empirical Social Work Practice*, vol. 1, John Wiley and Sons, Inc., New York, pp. 1-21.

Trinder, L. (1996), 'Social Work Research: The State of the Art (or Science)', *Child and Family Social Work*, vol. 1, pp. 233-242.

Tyson, K.B. (1992), 'A New Approach to Relevant Scientific Research for Practitioners: The Heuristic Paradigm', in *Social Work*, vol. 37, pp. 541-556.

Index